HANDS-ON GEOLOGY
AF538929
Get Hands-On With
Fossils!
Full of experiments and projects to help you learn all about fossils.
Alix Wood

Published and Distributed in India by Scholastic India Pvt. Ltd.

Produced for Rosen Publishing by Alix Wood Books
Designed and Illustrated by Alix Wood
Editor: Eloise Macgregor

Consultant: Kate Spencer, Professor of Environmental Geochemistry

Photo credits:
Cover, 3, 4, 6 all except 6 middle inset, 8, 12 bottom, 14, 15, 20 all except top, 23, 24 © Adobe Stock Images; 6 middle inset @ Denali National Park & Preserve, Alaska (public domain); 7 © Havardtl (public domain); 12 middle © Desert Museum, Saltillo (public domain); 20 top © needpix.com; all other photographic images are in the public domain

Cover, 33, 35, 36, 37, 40 top, 42, 44 top, 46, 47, 48, 49, 50, 52, 54, 56 top left, 57 top © AdobeStock Images; 40 bottom © Hans-Joachim Engelhardt; 42 bottom © James St. John; 45 metallic © JJ Harrison, glassy © Didier Descouens, resinous © Hannes Grobe, greasy © Ra'ike, pearly © Luis Miguel Bugallo Sánchez, brilliant © Robert M. Lavinsky, dull © Karla Panchuk; 56 top right © Alexander Van Driessche; 56 middle © Robert M. Lavinsky; 56 bottom © Malopolska's Virtual Museums Project

Illustrations © Alix Wood

Printed in India by Saurabh Printers Pvt. Ltd.
First edition: 2021
This Reprint Edition: May 2024

ISBN 978-93-5954-846-3

Contents

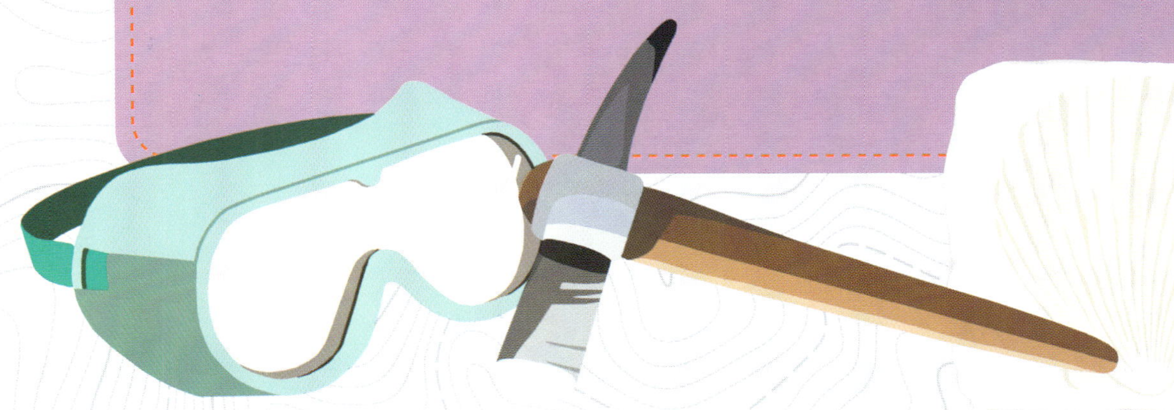

What Are Fossils?

Fossils are the remains or traces of plants and animals that lived long ago. If you have a rock collection, look closely. You may find tiny fossils, millions of years old, embedded in some of them. The word fossil comes from the Latin word "fossilis," which means "dug up."

the fossilized shell of an ammonite

Most of the fossils that we find come from areas that were once underwater. A type of rock that forms underwater, **sedimentary rock**, creates the perfect conditions for forming fossils. That is why most fossils are of sea creatures, or animals whose bodies fell into water.

How Fossils Form

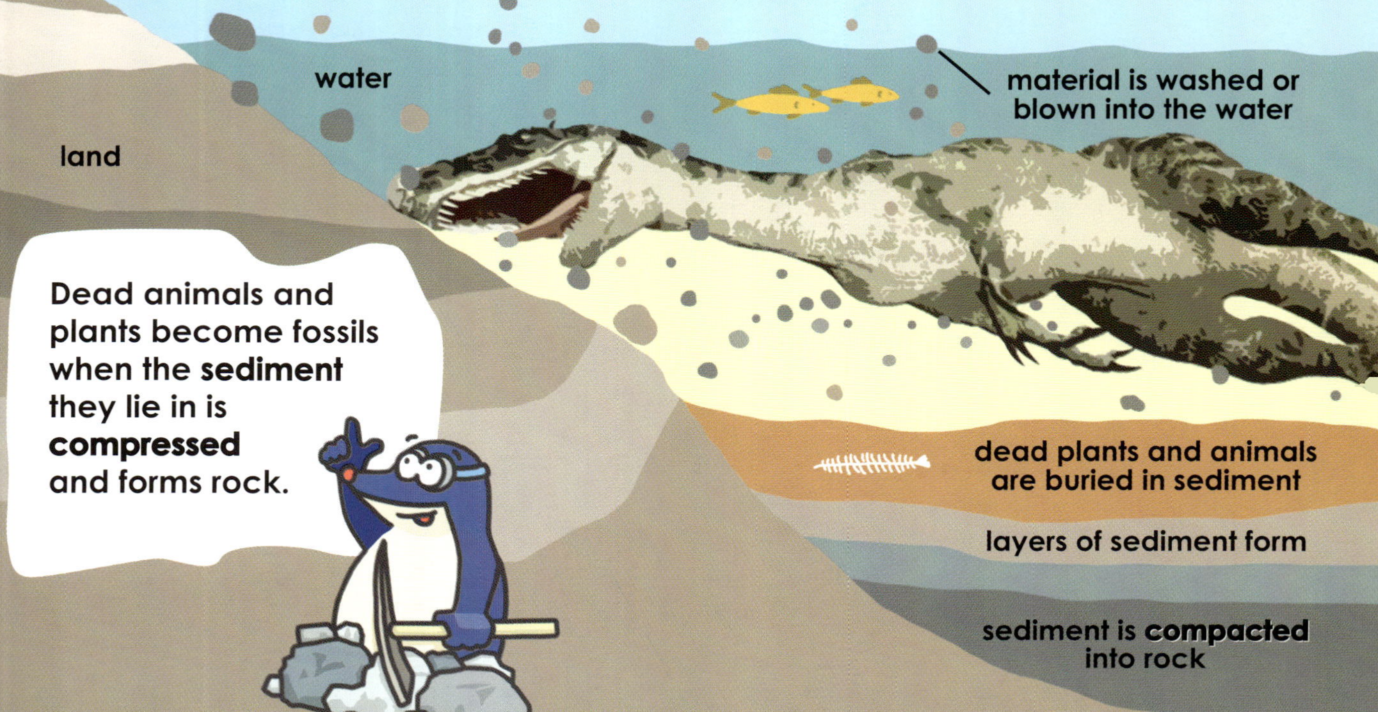

Dead animals and plants become fossils when the **sediment** they lie in is **compressed** and forms rock.

Why Study Fossils?

Fossils give scientists clues about the past. People who study fossils are called **paleontologists**. "Paleo" means ancient, and "ontology" is the study of existence. Paleontologist's discoveries have helped them piece together what Earth would have been like millions of years ago. Fossils help show what **extinct** animals looked like, where they lived, and why they may have become extinct. They also give clues about what Earth looked like long ago.

Think About This...

Long ago, Earth looked very different. Oceans covered areas that are now land. Some **continents** were joined together that now have an ocean between them. How do you think fossils helped scientists work that out?

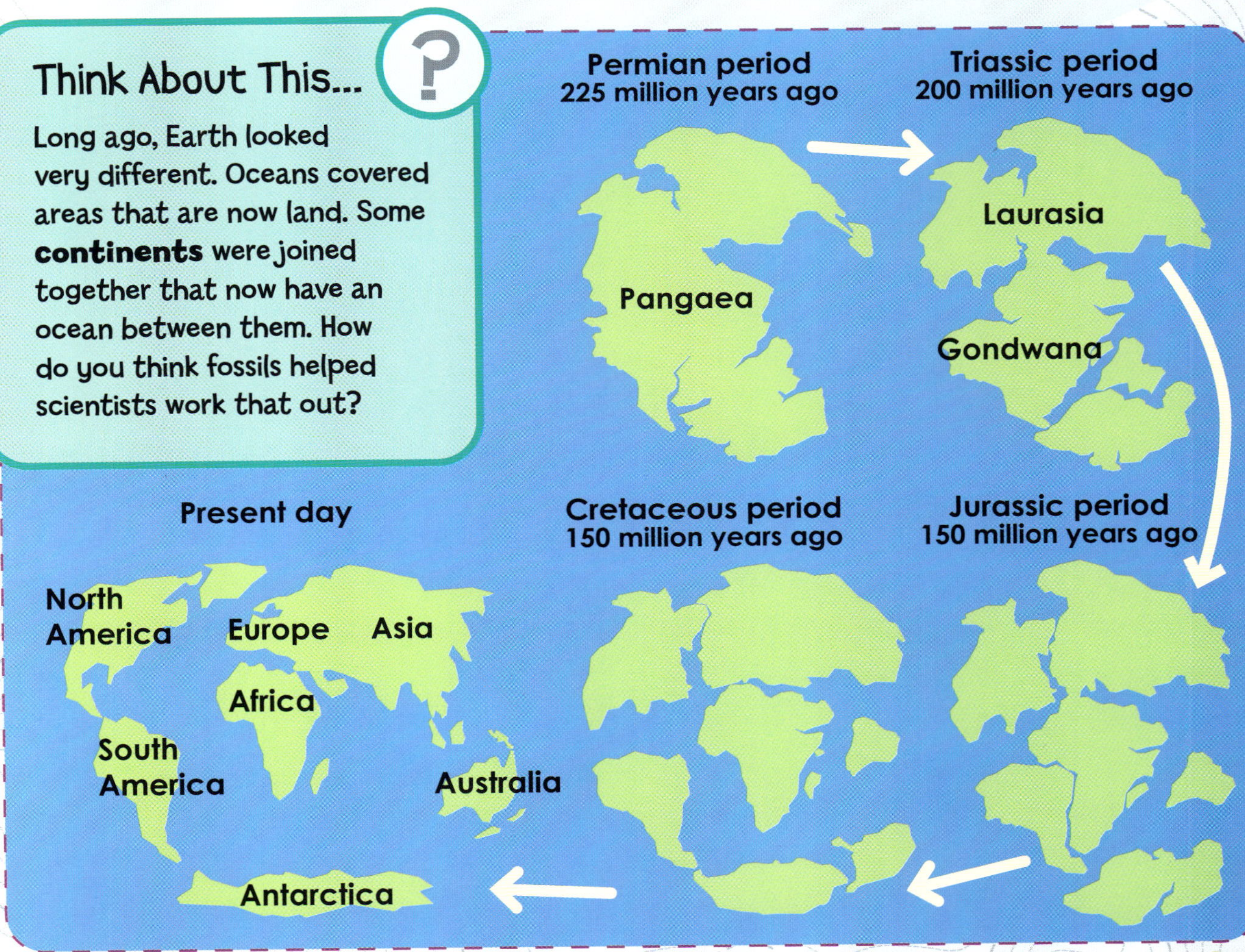

HANDS-ON Make a Continent Jigsaw

You Will Need:

- a map or globe
- thin paper
- pencil
- scissors

Trace the outlines of the present-day continents using a map or globe. Carefully cut them out. See how well you can fit the continents together. Do any still fit quite well? Can you make something that looks a little like Pangaea? Why do you think some continents might not fit well together any more?

Different Types Of Fossil

Animal and plant remains can turn into fossils in different ways. There are two main types of fossils; body fossils and trace fossils.

bones

Body Fossils

Body fossils are the remains of plants or animals that were once living. The soft parts of an animal's body usually rot away once it dies. But the hard parts; the teeth, claws, shell, and bones, might be preserved and eventually harden to rock.

Finding a complete dinosaur skeleton is rare. Usually, the bones have been scattered either by animals, the weather, or flowing water. The skulls, being hollow and lightweight, have often been crushed or are missing.

teeth

Teeth are covered in a substance called enamel that is harder than bone. Sometimes the teeth are the only part of a species of dinosaur that is ever found. Some dinosaurs, such as Megalosaurus, used to shed their teeth regularly and grow new ones. So, fossilized Megalosaurus teeth are quite common.

leaves

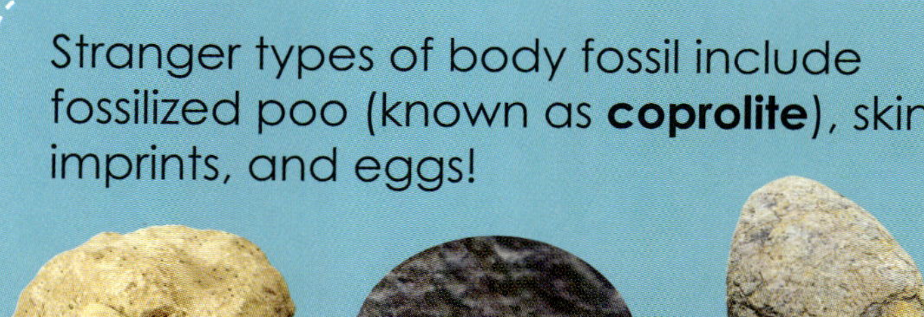

Stranger types of body fossil include fossilized poo (known as **coprolite**), skin imprints, and eggs!

poo

skin

egg

shells

Trace Fossils

Trace fossils are fossils of signs that a plant or animal lived, rather than fossils of the animal or plant itself. They are fascinating. Holes near bird tracks show birds used their beaks to find food. A burrow in the same rock may show what insect the birds were looking for!

These dinosaur tracks are a trace fossil.

Think About This...

Fossilization is so unlikely that less than one-tenth of one percent of animal species that ever lived have become fossils! How many do you think have actually been found?

BE A PALEONTOLOGIST
Make Your Own Trace Fossil

You Will Need:

- a cup of flour
- a cup of salt
- cup of water
- bowl
- spoon
- greased baking tray
- toy plastic dinosaur

The Geology:

Paleontologists can tell all kinds of things from dinosaur footprints. They can tell the speed the dinosaur ran, its size, the number of legs it had, and if the dinosaur traveled in groups.

How To Make Footprints

Put half the salt and all the flour into a bowl and mix together. Mix in the water a little at a time. Gradually add more salt until the mixture is not too sticky and feels like dough.

Roll the dough into a ball. Flatten it until around an inch (2.5 cm) thick and place it on the baking tray. Dip the dinosaur's feet in flour then press the feet into the dough. Leave to dry for a couple of days, or bake for 20 minutes at 350 degrees Fahrenheit.

The Perfect Conditions

Not every animal or plant that dies is turned into a fossil. The conditions have to be just right. Most fossils are formed by a process known as "mold and cast." When an animal or plant dies in sediment its body is dissolved by water seeping through the rock. As it dissolves it leaves a hollow mold where it lay. **Minerals** in the water fill the mold and replace the bone. This creates a rock **replica**, a little like a cast statue, of the original skeleton.

A fish dies and its body falls to the bottom of the water. After a while only its skeleton is left.

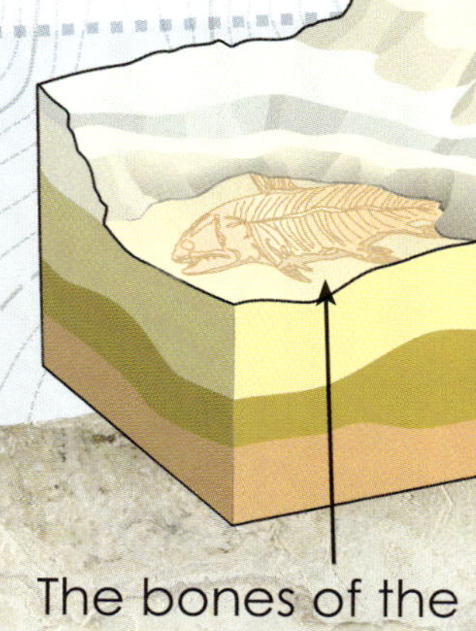

The bones of the skeleton create a hollow in the sediment.

The buried bones gradually dissolve, replaced by minerals that fill the hollow.

It can take millions of years for minerals in ground water to fill the mold. Eventually, the skeleton becomes solid rock. The fossil will remain underground until either the surrounding rock is worn away and exposes the fossil, or it is dug up by fossil hunters.

Think About This...

Why do you think fossilized worms are very rare?

BE A PALEONTOLOGIST

Make a Mold and Cast Fossil

You Will Need:

- small plastic or foil container
- modeling clay
- a shell (or a plastic dinosaur)
- petroleum jelly
- plaster of Paris
- a bowl and mixing spoon
- water
- rubber gloves, eye protection, and face mask

The Geology:

The modeling clay in this activity acts like the river bed.

Pressing the shell into the clay represents the dead animal making a hollow in the sediment. The animal gradually decays, leaving a mold of its original shape.

Removing the shell and filling the mold with plaster represents the minerals replacing the animal's body and forming the fossil.

How To Make Your Fossil

Knead the modeling clay until soft. Place a 1 inch (2.5 cm) deep layer of clay in the bottom of a small container. Smear your shell in petroleum jelly. This makes it easier to remove the shell once the plaster has set. Press the shell into the clay, then remove it carefully so the print doesn't smudge. If the shell won't come out, hold an edge and gently rock the shell back and forth.

Put on eye protection, gloves, and a face mask. Plaster of Paris can irritate your eyes, skin, and lungs. Measure the plaster into a bowl, following the instructions on the packet. Mix enough plaster to fill your mold and cover the clay. Using a spoon, mix the plaster with water until it is quite runny. Spoon the mixture into the mold. Smooth the plaster to form a flat surface and then let it dry for around 24 hours.

Turn the container upside-down. Gently press out the mold. Carefully peel the clay from the plaster. Now you have your very own fossil! Keep it safe - you'll use it again later.

How Does Sediment Turn To Rock?

Sediment is material, such as sand, minerals and the remains of plants and animals, that is washed, blown or moved by ice to areas such as river beds. How does sediment turn into rock? When sediment is compacted and **cemented** by great pressure, any liquid or gaps that existed in the sediment are pressed out. Sediment is gradually compressed so much that it becomes solid.

extreme pressure

This process of turning sediment to rock is known as **lithification.** "Lithos" means "rock" in Ancient Greek. Try the experiments on these pages to understand how lithification happens, and make your very own rock!

HANDS-ON Make a Jar of Sediment

You will need:

- dirt, soil, leaves, sand and pebbles
- a large jar with a lid
- some water
- a small plastic dinosaur

First, go outside and collect lots of different materials that might be found in sediment. For example, gather leaves, compost, soil, clay, small rocks, and sand.

Fill a jar three-quarters full of water. Put most of your collected dirt into the jar. Put on the lid, and shake the jar. You should see the water turn brown as the material mixes in with the water. As the dirt starts to settle try to guess which materials will sink, and which will float to the top.

Place your plastic dinosaur into the jar and watch where it settles. Does it sink below any of the layers? What happens if you sprinkle the rest of the mixture on top?

There are two processes that turn sediment into rock.

Compaction
The loose particles in sediment are squashed by their own weight, and the weight above them. Eventually, there is little or no empty space left between each particle.

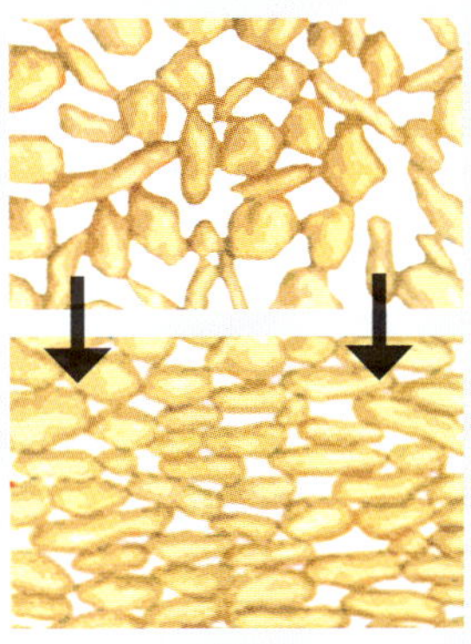

Cementation
When minerals crystallize in the spaces between particles and hold them tightly together.

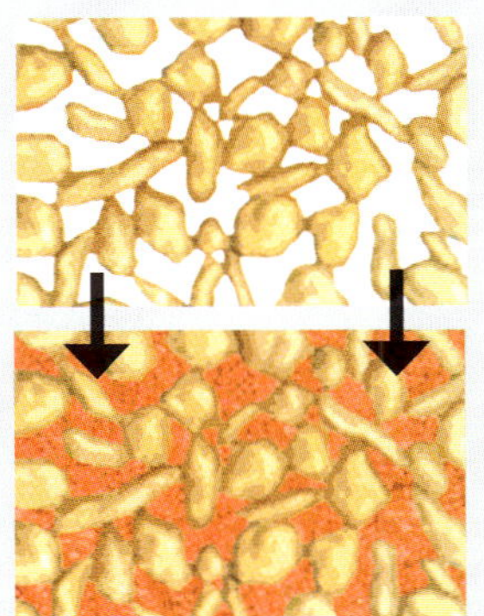

BE A PALEONTOLOGIST
Try Compaction and Cementation

You Will Need:

adult help needed

- sand
- water
- plaster of Paris
- scissors
- two small yogurt pots
- an old bowl and tablespoon
- eye protection, gloves, and face mask

The Geology:

Some sediment can be compacted to form rock. Sand and coarse-grained sediment needs a natural "cement" made from minerals to bind it. The chemicals that act as cement are found in **groundwater**. They are usually silica, calcium carbonate, or iron **compounds**.

How To Make Your Own Rock

Dampen some sand with water. Half fill a yogurt pot with the sand and press it down very firmly. Carefully cut away the plastic pot. You may need an adult to help you. Leave the compacted sand "rock" to dry.

Now repeat the same experiment, but this time instead of just using damp sand, mix in some "cement." Put on eye protection, gloves, and a face mask as plaster of Paris can irritate your eyes, skin, and lungs. In an old bowl, mix one tablespoon of plaster of Paris to four tablespoons of damp sand. Firmly press the sand into the yogurt pot. Then cut away the pot and leave your "rock" to dry.

Which process made the hardest "rock" from your sand, compaction or cementation?

Whole Animal Fossils

Not all fossils are found in sedimentary rock. Usually, when an animal dies, **bacteria** eats away at the soft parts of the body. However, bacteria do not like very cold or dry conditions. Animals that die in a desert cave or are quickly frozen in ice may be fossilized whole.

Whole animal fossils, like this fish, have been found in deserts, their bodies preserved by the dry air.

This baby wooly mammoth fossil was buried in mud and clay which quickly froze, preserving it. The stomach still had traces of its mother's milk. The mammoth died around 42,000 years ago!

Think About This...

What could paleontologists learn from a whole animal fossil that they couldn't tell from just bones and teeth.

Trapped!

When an animal becomes trapped in tree **resin**, its whole body may get preserved. When an insect lands on some sticky tree resin, it can become stuck. Over time, more resin falls on top of it. Over millions of years the resin hardens, and changes into a hard material called amber.

Whole dead animals and plants can become preserved in paraffin, and in a decaying plant matter known as peat, too.

a spider trapped in amber

BE A PALEONTOLOGIST
Make an Amber Fossil

You Will Need:

adult help needed

- clear nail polish
- modeling clay
- yellow and red food coloring
- some newspaper
- a small dead insect (or plastic toy insect)

Window sills or wood piles are a good place to find a dead insect. Never use an insect you think might be alive. If you can't find a dead insect, use a plastic one instead.

The Geology:

Nature is very good at getting rid of waste. Animals and plants **decompose** when they die. How? Bacteria break down the soft tissues. Some types of animals and birds, known as scavengers, will eat dead animals. Certain insects eat plant and animal waste, too. Weather and erosion can break down any bones and teeth that are left.

It is amazing that any whole body fossils have been found!

How To Make Your Fossil

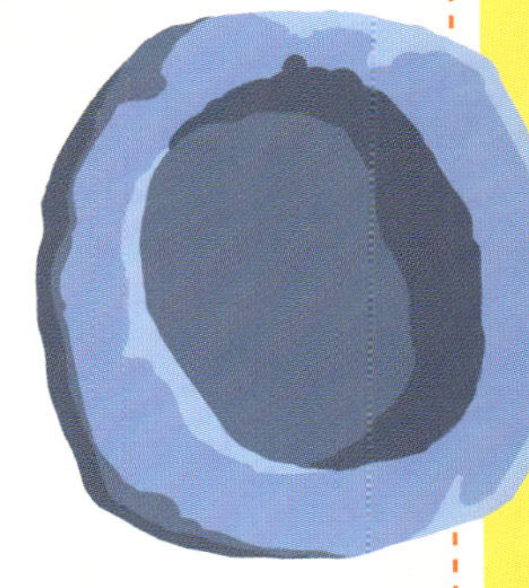

Roll a small ball of modeling clay. Press your thumb in the middle to make a hole large enough to fit your dead or toy insect. This will be your mold.

Ask an adult to help you, as nail polish and food color will stain. Cover a table with newspaper. Carefully open the nail polish. Put a few drops of yellow and one drop of red food coloring into the polish. Screw the lid on tightly and shake the mixture. It should now look amber-colored.

Pour a small amount of nail polish into the bottom of the clay mold you made. Place the insect in the hole.

Wait around 15 minutes for the polish to dry so it glues the insect in place. Then gradually add more layers of polish, a little at a time. Let it dry between each layer. When the insect is fully covered, leave your mold to dry for a few hours. When it is completely dry, peel the modeling clay away from your "amber" fossil.

More Amazing Fossils

Paleontologists can answer a lot of questions about ancient times by examining puzzling fossils. For example, what are the smooth, strange rocks sometimes found near dinosaur skeletons? Was the Arizona desert once really a forest?

A Fossil Forest

All plants, even huge trees, can become fossils. **Petrified** wood is wood that has turned to stone. Just as with animal bones, minerals in water can preserve trees buried in **volcanic** ash or sediment, replacing the wood to form fossils. If you look closely at a piece of petrified wood you might see tree rings, bark and maybe even insects that had burrowed into the wood.

Huge chunks of petrified trees can be found at the Petrified Forest National Park in Arizona. The fossils are an ancient type of conifer tree common when dinosaurs roamed the Earth. Some of the giant trees are thought to have been over 164 feet (50 meters) tall!

Different minerals create different color fossils. Iron has turned this wood red and orange. Manganese creates blue, purple, and black fossils. Copper can turn them green.

Using Rocks As Teeth!

Some dinosaurs swallowed rocks to help them digest their food. As the dinosaurs did not have grinding teeth, they used the rocks to grind food in a special area of their stomach. These smoothed stones, known as **gastroliths**, have been found in, or near, dinosaur fossils.

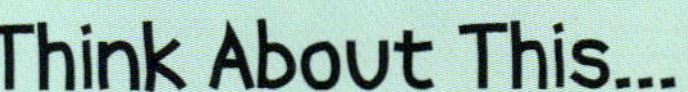

Think About This...

Can you think of any modern animals that use rocks to digest their food?

BE A PALEONTOLOGIST
Gastroliths? Examine the Evidence

The Geology:

Geologists need several pieces of **evidence** before they can be sure that a rock is a dinosaur gastrolith.

- The rock must be unlike other rock nearby. This shows the dinosaur traveled to the area with the gastrolith in its stomach.
- The rock should be rounded and polished. A gastrolith would have rubbed against other stones and material and become smooth.
- The stone must be found with, or near, the fossil of the dinosaur that swallowed it.

Asking the Questions

Study the photograph of the dinosaur fossil above.

- Can you see any rocks that might be gastroliths?
- Are they in or near the skeleton of the dinosaur?
- Are they in or near where the stomach might have been?
- Are there any rocks that look similar nearby?
- If you can see gastroliths, are they smooth and rounded?

Where Can You Find Fossils?

To have a chance of finding fossils, you need to find the right kind of rock. Most fossils are found in sedimentary rock. Fossil hunters look for areas of sedimentary rock that have either risen to the surface, or where the surrounding rock has worn away. Sedimentary rock is usually formed in water, so some of the best places to look are near water, where water used to be, or where rock has been worn away.

Useful things to have when fossil hunting

- Toilet paper to wrap any fossils in
- Food bags and a backpack to carry them home
- A small shovel, geology hammer, chisel, and eye protection
- A field journal and pen for recording your finds
- Plenty of water
- A phone in case you get into difficulty

Do

Only fossil hunt where it is okay to collect fossils. Check with an adult if you're not sure.

Stay away from cliff edges.

Keep an eye on the tides.

Beware of sinking sand or mud.

Wear eye protection in case rock fragments hit your face.

If you find a really interesting fossil, leave it, note where it is, and let a museum know.

Don't

Never go fossil-hunting alone.

Don't climb or wander into dangerous areas.

Never touch unknown animals – they might be poisonous.

Don't hammer at cliffs – it can cause a rockfall.

Don't try to take large fossils. Photograph them instead, so others can enjoy them, too.

HANDS-ON Planning a Fossil Hunt

You will need:

adult help needed

- access to a computer
- maps of the area

Remember – Never fossil hunt alone. Decide where would be the best place to search, and tell someone where you are going before your group set off.

Visit local museums and visitor centers, or search for local fossil hunter clubs or rock shops. These places will help you learn which fossils are common in the area, so you can recognise any fossils you might find. Ask an adult to help you search the internet for information on local fossils. Look at maps of the area. **Geological maps** will show you where each different type of rock can be found.

BE A PALEONTOLOGIST
Keeping a Fossil Hunt Field Journal

You Will Need:

- a notebook
- a pencil

How To Keep Records

It is easy to forget the details of a find once you get home. Make sure you have your journal with you on your fossil hunt. Note down all the facts about your discovery.

The Geology:

Fossil hunters note down details of their finds. It is important to record things like the kind of rock the fossil was found in, how deep underground the fossil was, and if there were any other fossils near by. This may help paleontologists work out where and when the animal lived, what it ate, and how it died.

Date: May 27th 2021, early morning
Fossil hunters: Iain and Rebecca
Place: Linton Marshes
Find: ammonite
Special comments: the ammonite was on the surface of a steep slope, in a layer of what looked like limestone. The rock was soft and broke away easily.

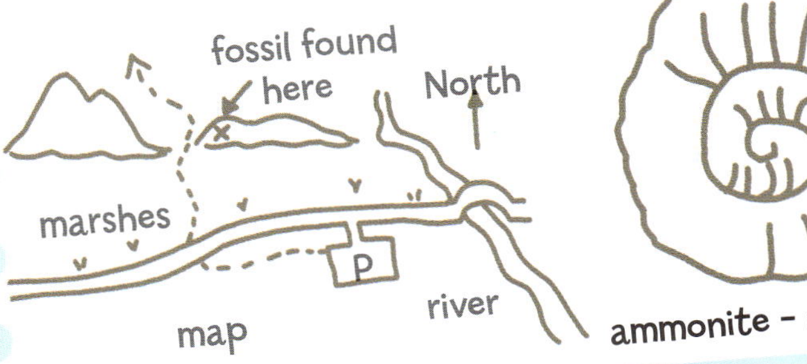

How The Experts Dig Up Fossils

As fossilization is rare, each fossil can hold vital information about prehistoric times. If you find an interesting fossil, especially an animal fossil, contact a museum for help before you try to excavate it. Why? There are many reasons why it is often better NOT to excavate a fossil:

- It's easy to damage a fossil during excavation. You may lose the information it could have provided.
- Removing a fossil takes it away from its **context**. Context is the fossil's surroundings, which give paleontologists information about where it lived, what it ate, and what other species were around at the same time.
- You might find bones of several animals. Leaving the fossils in place makes it easier for an expert to tell which bones belong to which animal.

Paleontologists will make notes and draw sketches of the site.

These are some of the tools a paleontologist might take to a dig.

brushes and dental picks

a geological hammer

a tape measure

Geological hammers have a flat face at one end for breaking rock. At the other end they either have a chisel or a pointed tip for cutting and picking out the rock.

HANDS-ON Try Excavating

It is useful to take photographs of the site at different stages of the excavation.

You will need:

- paintbrushes
- a toothpick
- a spoon
- eye protection
- gloves
- spray bottle
- some water

See if you can carefully excavate the mold and cast fossil you made on page 9. Imagine the surrounding material is the sedimentary rock at your excavation site. To take the fossil back to your museum, you are going to have to carefully brush and pick away the surrounding rock. Can you manage to do it without breaking your fossil?

Try spraying the surrounding rock with water and then gradually pick and brush it away using your tools.

fossil

surrounding rock

Fossils can be so brittle they would shatter if you tried to remove them. Paleontologists soak the bone in a thin glue. Once dry, this holds the fossil together enough to let them remove it.

Paleontologists use paintbrushes and dental picks to slowly remove the surrounding rock. They might soften the sediment by lightly spraying it with water.

Fossil Identification

How do you know if you have found a fossil? If the area you found your specimen in is known for fossils, there is a chance your specimen might be one. Fossils, like this dinosaur bone pictured, are usually a different color and smoother than the surrounding rock.

If paleontologists think they've found a dinosaur bone, they might lick it! Fossil bones have tiny holes which cause them to stick to the tongue slightly. But don't you try it!

Some common fossils:

Ammonite

Ammonite molluscs lived in the sea and are one of the most common fossils. They have spiral shells, usually with ridges. There were more than 10,000 species of ammonite!

Brachiopods

Brachiopods are marine animals that still exist today. Their fossilized shells can be brown, gray, black, or white depending on the rock they are preserved in.

Corals

Corals are related to jellyfish and anemones and most live in warm, shallow seas. Finding coral fossils shows us the area must once have been warm sea.

Crinoids

Crinoids are related to starfish and appeared in the seas about 300 million years before dinosaurs! They look a little like flowers with ridged stems.

Echinoids

Echinoids are sea urchins. They have lived in the seas for 450 million years. Echinoid's long spine fossils are found more often than their brittle shells.

Trilobites

Trilobites are bug-like creatures. Their name means "three lobes" as their bodies are divided into three. They became extinct about 250 million years ago.

BE A PALEONTOLOGIST
What Can a Fossil Skeleton Tell You?

Examining a Skeleton

Write down everything you know about chickens. You might say they have beaks and wings, eat worms, are covered in feathers, and walk on two legs? Look at the drawing of the chicken skeleton on the right. How many of those things can you tell from the skeleton alone?

Look at the dinosaur skeleton drawing, below. Can you answer these questions just by looking at the skeleton?

- Did it eat meat or plants?
- Do you think it could run fast?
- Did it walk on two or four legs?
- Do you think it had a large brain?

Which type of dinosaur do you think it is?

The Geology:

Paleontologists can tell a lot about a dinosaur from its skeleton. This dinosaur's sharp teeth show it mostly ate meat. Strong back legs hint that it could run fast. It probably used its short front legs for holding prey. The skull size hints it had a quite large brain. But–the skeleton can't show if it was covered in feathers. Or what color it was. Or if it had scales.

Think About This...

Can you see similarities between the chicken and Tyrannosaurus rex skeleton?

Travel Through Time

When was the first sign of life on Earth? How long ago did dinosaurs wander on our planet? When did the first humans live? To help answer these questions, paleontologists use a time scale known as **geologic time**. Geologic time is like a calendar of Earth's geologic history since it began. Geologic time starts around 4 **billion** years ago, when the Earth's crust was formed. How do we know it was formed then? The very oldest rock that geologists have found is about 4 billion years old.

BE A PALEONTOLOGIST
Make a Geologic Time line Clock

You Will Need:

- a plate to draw around
- paper
- scissors
- a pencil and ruler
- colored pencils

The Geology:

The only life-forms that existed in the whole of the Precambrian **era** were bacteria, jellyfish, and algae! Most of the fossils that we find are from the more recent Paleozoic, Mesozoic, and Cenozoic eras. The chart on the next page shows all the creatures that lived during these later eras.

How To Keep Records

If you imagine all of geologic time was compressed into just 12 hours, this geological clock shows how long each era lasted. Draw around a plate on a piece of paper. Cut out the circle. Fold it in half, and then into quarters. Open it out. Write the 3, 6, 9 and 12 on your clock at the folds. Then add the other numbers. Draw lines from the center of the circle to the points of the clock, as shown. Now color and label your time line.

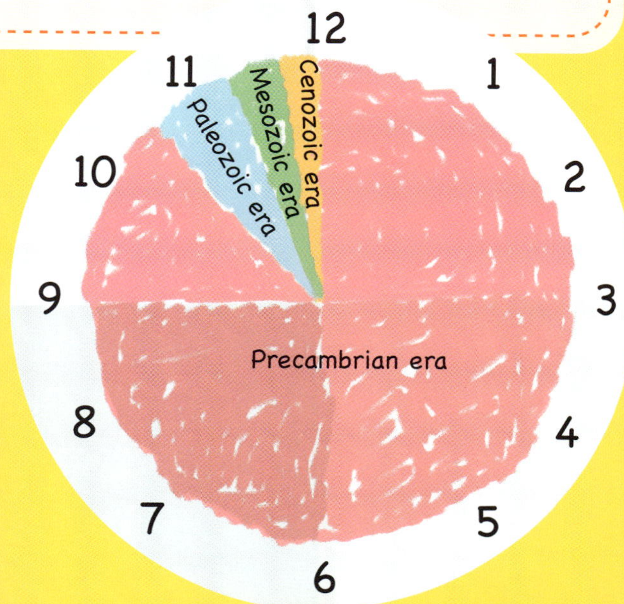

This geologic timeline shows the fossils we might find from the four main eras. The eras are divided into periods. "MYA" stands for "millions of years ago".

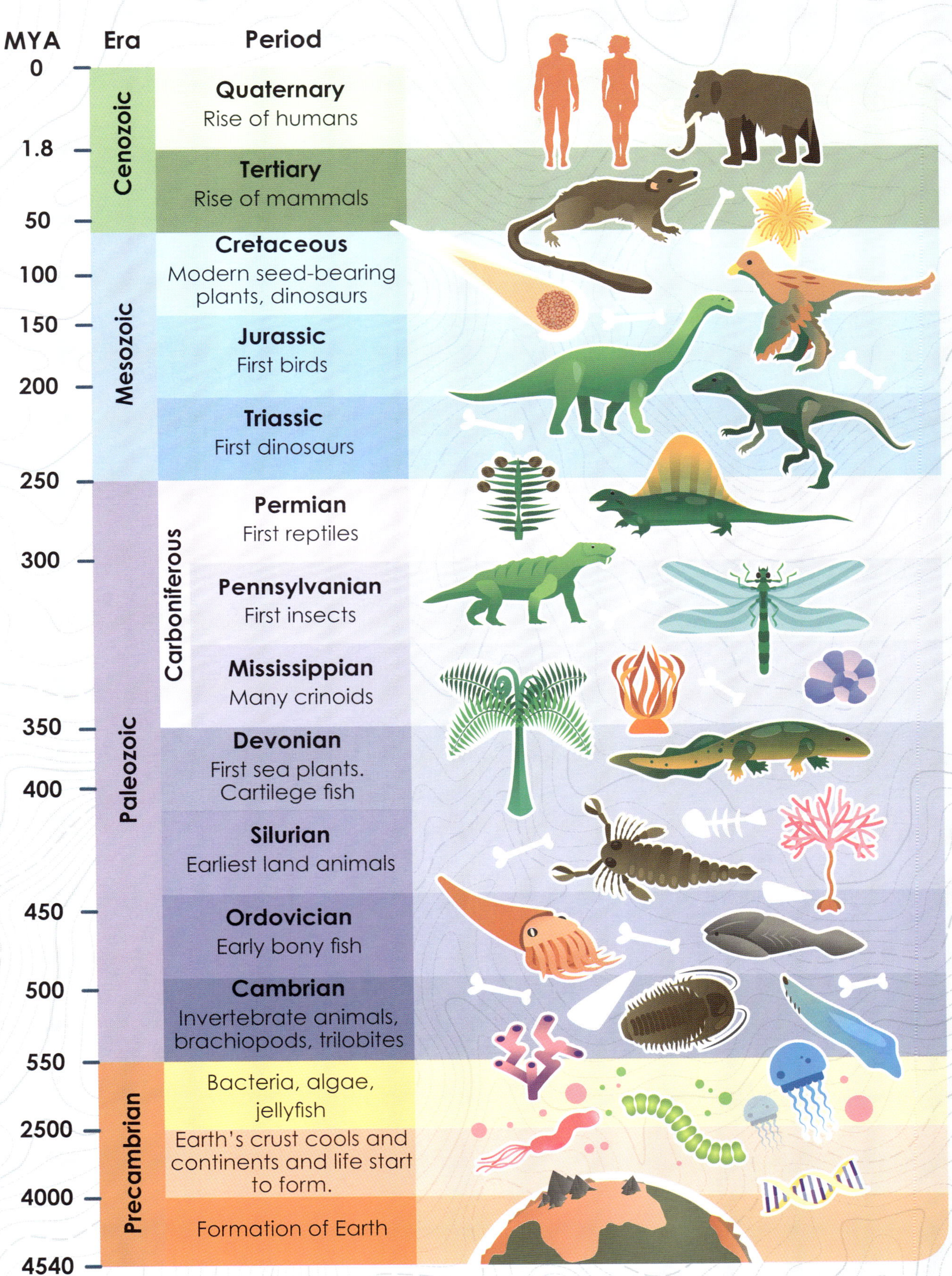

How Old Is My Fossil?

Dating fossils is not easy. There are three main ways scientists use. They either work out how old the rock layer the fossil was found in is. Or, they study materials in the fossil itself using methods such as **carbon dating**. Or, they study magnetic minerals in the rocks. Earth's magnetic field has changed through time and this can leave clues to a fossil's age.

If a fossil is found in a dark cave, a special meter can show paleontologists when the buried sediment last saw daylight.

Carbon and Uranium

A type of carbon in all living things decays at a particular rate once something dies. Scientists work out how long ago an animal died by examining the fossil's carbon. Some **elements** such as **uranium**, are **radioactive**. Over time, they become less radioactive. Paleontologists can measure this decay in any uranium-containing rock to work out how old a fossil is.

Think About This...

Fossils do not occur in rock that contains uranium. How does knowing how old that rock is help date the fossil layers?

HANDS-ON Dating Things Using Layers

You will need:

- a pencil
- some paper
- laundry basket

Ask your family to not do laundry for a week. Write the days of the week on pieces of paper. On Monday, hide the Monday note in the clothes you put in the laundry. Do the same for each day of the week. On Sunday, amaze your family by telling them what they wore each day. Use the hidden notes in your layers as clues. Remember to take the notes out, so they don't end up in the wash!

If paleontologists can't easily date a rock layer, they try to find other fossils in the same layer that can help them. Known as index fossils, certain fossils were only alive at a particular period. Finding an index fossil near the fossil they want to date is very helpful. Ammonites and trilobites make good index fossils because they are common, and different species lived during distinct time periods. Can you see the different patterns in the shells of the ammonite fossils below?

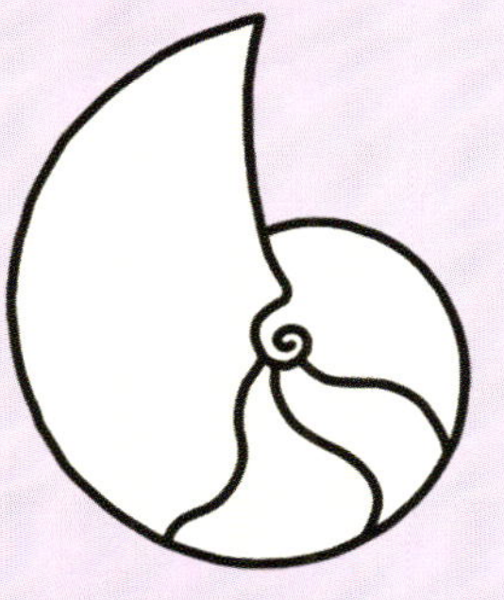

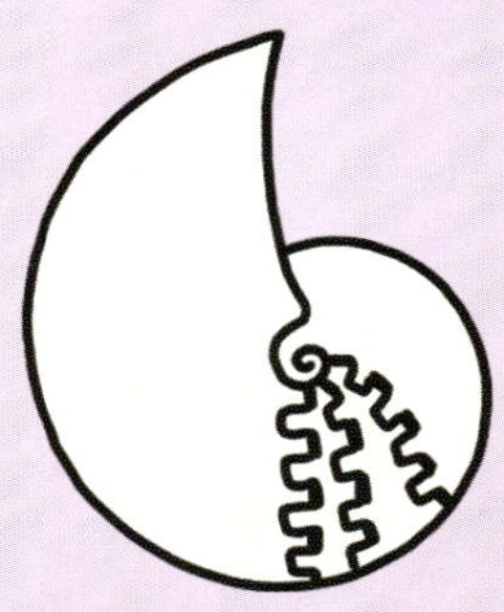

BE A PALEONTOLOGIST

Date a Dinosaur Using Index Fossils

You Will Need:

- a deep container
- soil
- paper and pen
- scissors
- four plastic dinosaurs
- some tape
- a friend

The Geology:

Ammonite shells have chambers that have joins between them known as sutures. The shell suture pattern tended to get more complicated over time. So, the less wiggly the sutures on an ammonite fossil are, the older the fossil probably is.

Asking the Questions

Design four ammonites. You could copy the ones pictured above. Draw each one on a separate piece of paper. Tape one ammonite to each plastic dinosaur. Decide what time period each ammonite lived in. Make a chart, with a picture of each ammonite next to its time period.

Permian

Triassic

Jurassic

Cretaceous

Put some soil in the bottom of your container. Put the oldest dinosaur and ammonite in the soil. Then add a second layer of soil, and the next oldest dinosaur and ammonite. Repeat until you have buried all four. Ask a friend to excavate the dinosaurs. Can they work out how old they are using your chart.

Using Maps To Help Find Fossils

Before setting out on a fossil-hunting expedition, paleontologists will usually look at a geological map. A geological map shows the age and type of rocks in an area. Studying a map first means they will not waste time looking in areas with the wrong rock. Fossil hunters don't just look for a particular type of rock. The rock also needs to be the right age for the fossils they are looking for.

Most fossils are found in sedimentary rock. Dinosaur fossils are found in sedimentary rock that was formed in the Mesozoic era.

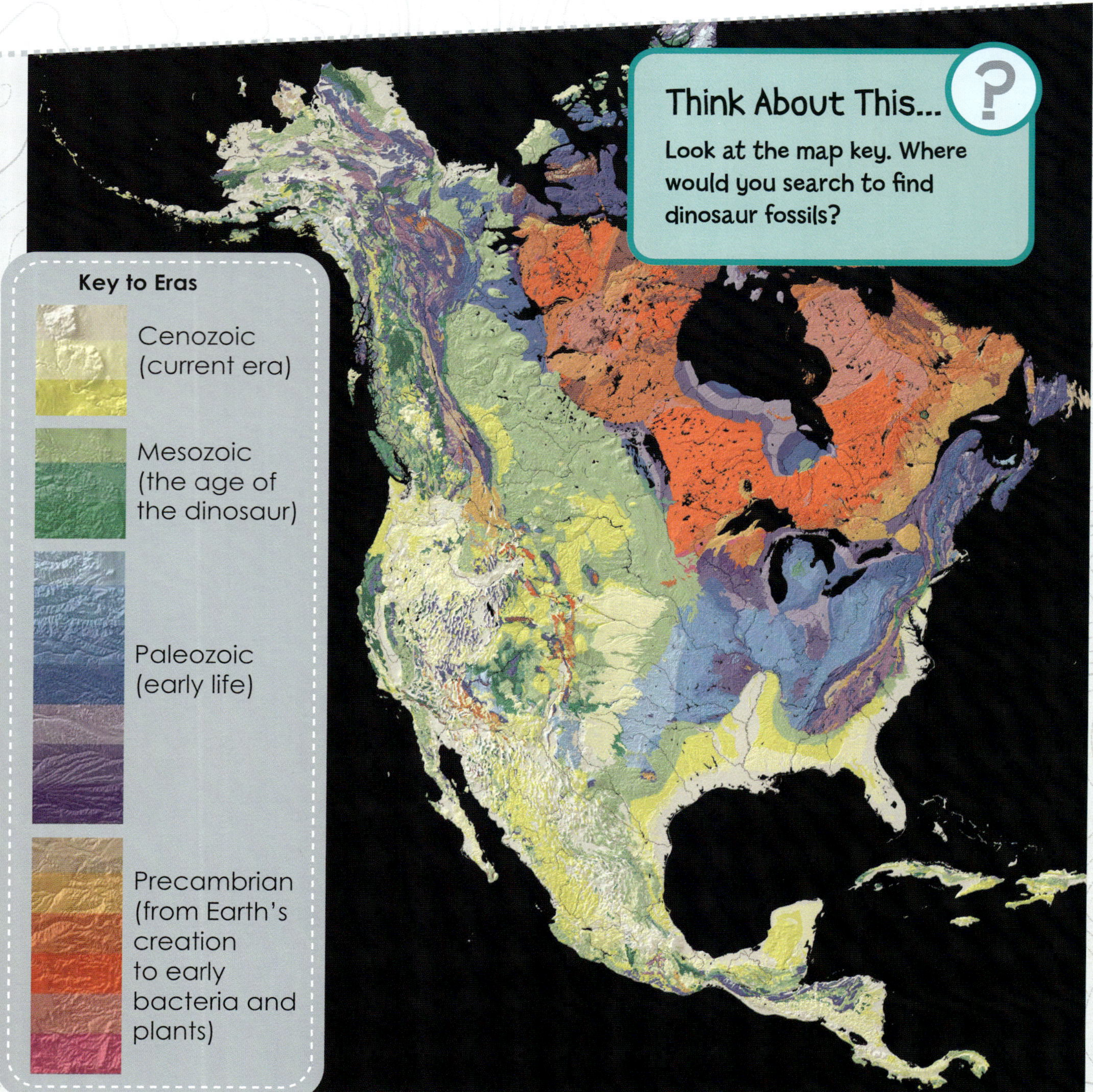

Think About This...

Look at the map key. Where would you search to find dinosaur fossils?

BE A PALEONTOLOGIST
Make a Geological Map of Your Area

You Will Need:

- paper
- colored pencils or crayons
- greaseproof or tracing paper
- some tape
- a ruler

The Geology:

Map makers use aerial photographs and surveys to create their base maps. They find out how old the rock is in the same way as they age fossils.

If you want to find Tyrannosaurus rex fossils, look for exposed rock around 65 million years old. If you want to find a trilobite, you need even older rock, more than 245 million years old. Once you find the right rock, finding a fossil still needs a bit of luck, too.

How To Make Your Map

Make a basic outline of the area you want to map. Perhaps draw your yard, or street. Tape a sheet of tracing paper along one edge, so it flaps over your drawing. Draw a grid on this layer, dividing your map into squares. Try to get each square of your map around a pace apart in real life.

With your map as reference, go to each area of your grid. Dig up a tiny bit of soil. What is it like? Can you roll it into a ball - then it is probably clay. Is it gritty like sand? Or is it dark with woody bits like compost? Perhaps you found large areas of gray solid rock, or small pebbles, or lighter, sandy rock? Look up some information on rocks and see if you can identify them.

Make a key for your map. Give each soil or rock type a different color. Mark each grid square with the correct color spots.

Sharing The Knowledge

You can find information about fossils at some local museums. They may have local area geological maps and examples of fossils that have been found in your area, too. In areas well-known for fossils, there are often groups where people with an interest in fossils meet and give talks. They may be happy to help you identify fossils that you find, too.

To stay safe, make sure you ask your parents or caregivers to help you contact a group, and to come along with you.

BE A PALEONTOLOGIST
Make Your Own Fossil Exhibit

You Will Need:

- some fossils
- paper and pen
- information leaflets
- a table
- some wall space
- the projects you made in this book

Setting Up Your Display

It's fun to create your own museum display. Gather together any fossils that you have and place them on a table. You could display them in boxes if they are very small. Put labels next to each fossil with as much information as you can. You could put where you found or bought it, what you think it might be, and how old you think it is.

MORE IDEAS - Make some posters to go on the wall that tell visitors all about fossils. Put out any tools that you used to excavate them. You could try drawing some dinosaurs and other ancient animals, too. Display your geological map and trace fossil, if you made them. Challenge visitors to date fossils using your index ammonites.

This way to the Fossil Museum

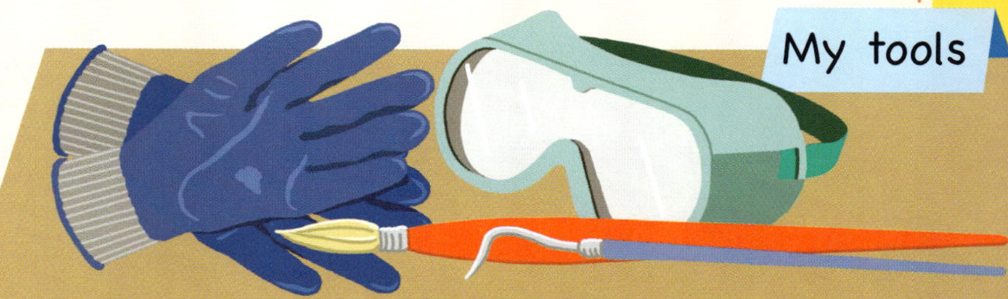

HANDS-ON Create a Dinosaur Landscape

You will need:

- a large tray or bowl
- some toy dinosaurs
- some small plants
- soil or sand
- rocks and pebbles

Create your own model of a prehistoric scene. Put a layer of sand or soil into a tray. Place some rocks and pebbles around your landscape. Push some small plants into the soil. Add your toy dinosaurs. You could display your model in your museum.

Why not photocopy a dinosaur skeleton and ask visitors to design what it might have looked like. What color was it? Did it have skin, hair, scales, or feathers?

Make some tickets to hand out at the door. You could write a small guide explaining your exhibits and give visitors the guide when they arrive. Maybe make a quiz for visitors to do, to see if they have learnt anything from your exhibits! Once you are all set up, invite your friends and family to come and visit your museum.

The Geology:

It's great to share knowledge with other fossil-hunters. Everyone can learn from everyone else. Because some fossils are quite rare it is important to share the ones you have found. They could hold important information that no one has ever found before!

Model fossils

Glossary

bacteria any of a group of single-celled microorganisms that live in soil, water, the bodies of plants and animals.

billion a thousand million, written 1,000,000,000.

carbon dating the measurement of age (as of a fossil) by means of the amount of carbon-14 in the material.

cemented united by or as if by cement.

cementation when minerals crystallize in the spaces between particles and hold them tightly together.

compacted made or become compact.

compaction when loose particles in sediment are squashed until there is little or no empty space left between each particle.

compounds substances formed by the union of two or more chemical elements.

compressed reduced the size, amount, or volume by pressure.

context the setting for an event, idea, or statement by which it can be fully understood.

continents one of the great divisions of land on the globe.

coprolite fossilized poop.

decompose to break down an organism through biological activity (for example by bacteria) into simpler chemical substances.

era one of the five major divisions of geologic time.

elements fundamental substances that consist of atoms of only one kind and that cannot be separated into simpler substances.

evidence available facts or information indicating whether a belief is true.

extinct no longer existing.

gastroliths a small stone swallowed by a bird, reptile, or fish to aid digestion.

geological maps special-purpose maps made to show various geological features.

geologic time the long period of time occupied by Earth's geologic history.

groundwater the water found underground in the cracks and spaces in soil, sand and rock.

lithification the process by which materials are converted into solid rock, as by compaction or cementation.

minerals solid chemical compounds that occur naturally in the form of crystals.

paleontologists scientists who study fossils.

paraffin a soft colorless solid derived from petroleum, coal or shale oil.

petrified converted into stone through a slow process of mineralization.

radioactive having or producing the energy that comes from the breaking up of atoms.

replica an exact copy of an object.

resin sticky yellow or brownish substance obtained from the gum or sap of some trees.

sediment material such as stones and sand deposited by water, wind, or glaciers.

sedimentary rock rock formed by or from sediment.

uranium a chemical element, a dense grey radioactive metal used as a fuel in nuclear reactors.

volcanic relating to, or produced by a volcano.

Further Information

Museums and Places to Visit

Visit a museum. Most big city museums will have some fossil exhibits, workshops, and information about local finds.

Visit local rock shops. You can usually find some interesting fossils to look at or buy.

Look for fossil-hunting clubs or groups. Some areas, especially areas that are well-known for fossils, will have clubs or groups you can join.

Useful Websites

This OneGeology site has all kinds of information about fossils and dinosaurs.
http://www.onegeology.org/extra/kids/fossils.html

The Natural History Museum features a cartoon showing how fossils are formed, and plenty of other great information, too.
https://www.nhm.ac.uk/discover/how-are-fossils-formed.html

The American Museum of Natural History website is packed with facts about fossils.
https://www.amnh.org/dinosaurs/dinosaur-facts

Books to Read

Lynch, Dan R. *Fossils for Kids: Finding, Identifying, and Collecting*. Cambridge, MA: Adventure Publications, 2020.

Morgan, Ben. *Eyewitness Explorer: Rock and Fossil Hunter: Explore Nature with Loads of Fun Activities*. New York, NY: DK Children, 2015.

Index

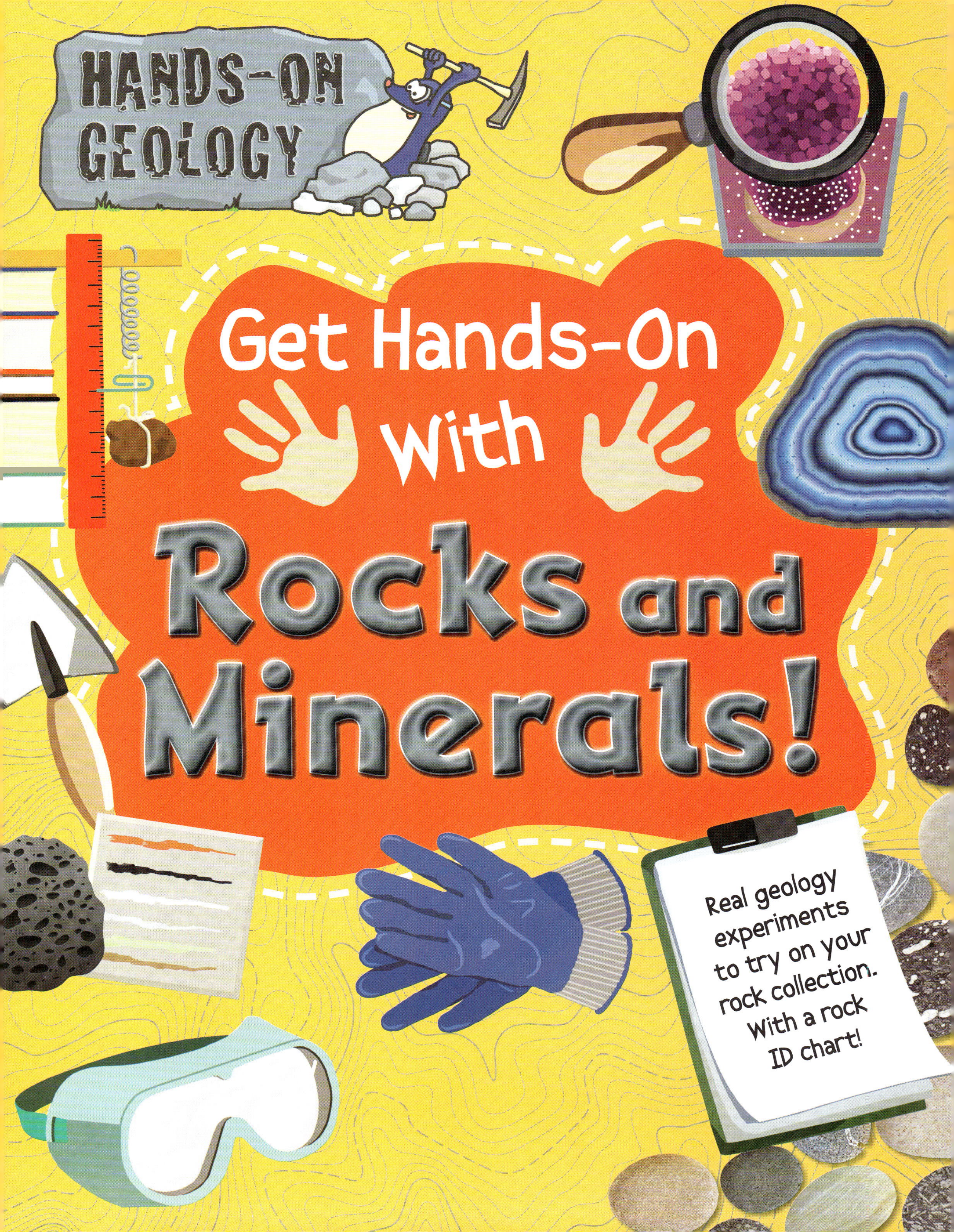
HANDS-ON GEOLOGY
Get Hands-On With
Rocks and Minerals!
Real geology experiments to try on your rock collection. With a rock ID chart!

Contents

What Exactly Is Rock?

Our planet, Earth, is made up of many layers. Rocks are the dry, solid material that make up the outer layer of Earth, known as the Earth's **crust**. If you go outside and look around, you are pretty sure to find some rock. Anything from a huge boulder to a grain of sand can be described as rock.

Broken rock, sand, and soil lie on the surface of the Earth's crust. The lower part of the crust is solid rock. Underneath Earth's crust is a layer called the **mantle**. The mantle is mainly solid rock, with areas where the rock has melted from the extreme heat of the Earth's **core**. As you head further toward the center of Earth, scientists believe the outer core is mainly liquid iron. The outer core surrounds a solid, mainly iron, inner core.

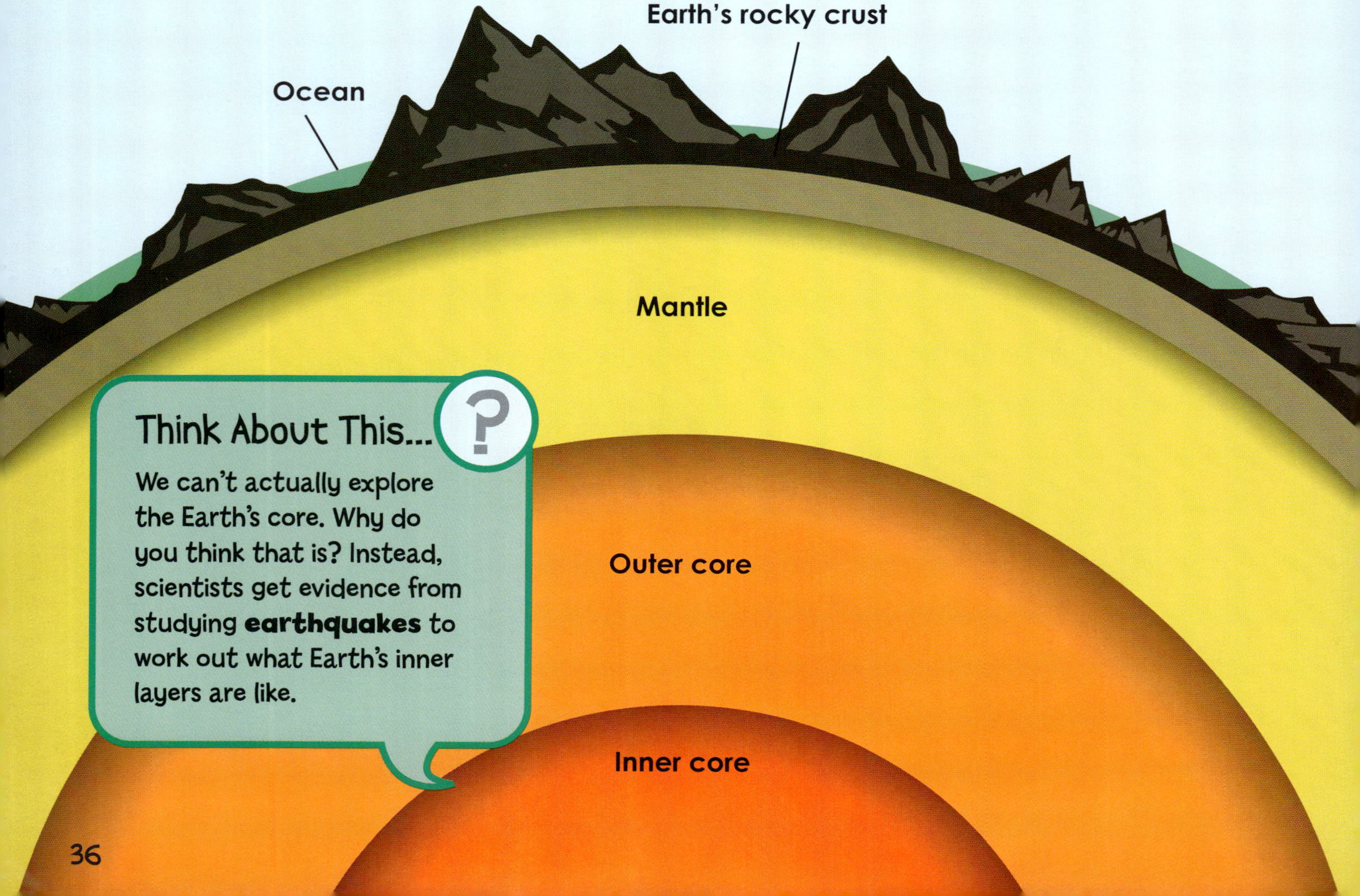

Earth's rocky crust

Ocean

Mantle

Outer core

Inner core

Think About This...

We can't actually explore the Earth's core. Why do you think that is? Instead, scientists get evidence from studying **earthquakes** to work out what Earth's inner layers are like.

Why Study Rocks?

Rock are fascinating. They have been around since Earth was formed. The study of rocks is called **geology**. People who study rocks are called geologists. Rocks give us clues about what Earth was like long before people lived on the planet. Studying an area's rocks can tell geologists if there was once a lake or **volcano** there, or if it was under the sea, or part of a mountain range, and even what the temperatures were like.

Studying rocks helps geologists learn about volcanoes and earthquakes, and predict where they might happen in the future. Fossils found in rocks give information about plants and animals that existed long ago. Studying an area's rocks can help find useful resources such as gold, or jewels, or oil.

HANDS-ON Go Rock Collecting

You Will Need:

- a bag or backpack to carry your rocks home

You May Want:

- gloves
- a rock hammer or pick
- eye protection
- a magnifying glass or hand lens

You may already have a rock collection. If not, start hunting. If you tell people about your hobby, other collectors might give you some of their spare rocks. Search your yard, and your neighborhood. See how many different rocks you can find.

Check you can take rocks from the area first. It can be illegal to remove rocks, particularly from beaches or streams. Why? Rocks and pebbles help protect coasts and riverbanks from erosion. If every visitor took one pebble, that may be enough to cause damage. Many creatures hide under rocks, too, so removing them may make them homeless.

ALWAYS wear eye protection when using a rock hammer. Small pieces of flying rock can hit you.

What Are Rocks Made Of?

Rocks are made up of **minerals**. Minerals are **inorganic** substances. Inorganic means not coming from a plant or an animal. Minerals are not made by people, either. They are found naturally in the Earth. Each mineral is made of a particular mix of **elements**. **Atoms** in these elements are arranged in a particular way, forming structures known as **crystals**.

Think About This...

"In" or "im" at the beginning of a word often means "not." Organic means coming from an animal or plant, so inorganic means not coming from an animal or plant. Can you think of any other words like that, that start with "in" or "im."

There are over 2,000 different minerals. Minerals can be all different colors, shapes, and sizes. Minerals are made from elements.

What Are Elements?

Elements are simple substances that cannot be broken down any further. For example, the mineral, pyrite, is made up of the elements iron and sulfur. You can break pyrite down into these two elements, but you cannot break those elements down further.

What Are Crystals?

Crystals form when a mineral's atoms fit together in a repeating pattern. Atoms are tiny particles that contain a mineral's chemical properties.

Kaolinite, a type of clay, has atoms that form sheets of crystals. The sheets slide over one another, making kaolinite feel slippy.

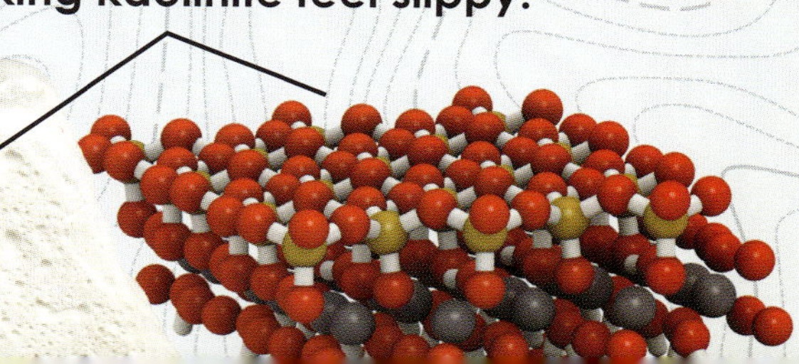

HANDS-ON Organize Your Rock Collection

You will need:

- some interesting rocks
- an old toothbrush
- paper and a pen
- some tape

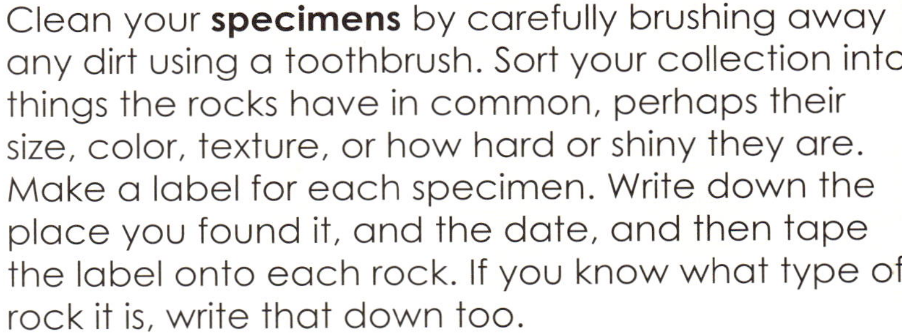

Clean your **specimens** by carefully brushing away any dirt using a toothbrush. Sort your collection into things the rocks have in common, perhaps their size, color, texture, or how hard or shiny they are. Make a label for each specimen. Write down the place you found it, and the date, and then tape the label onto each rock. If you know what type of rock it is, write that down too.

If you buy a rock, it's a good idea to keep any old labels. Rock collectors often note the name of the mine a rock was dug from, and the depth it was found at. They might write the price they paid for a rock, and any history they have found out about it.

BE A ROCK DETECTIVE
Make a Rock Identification Chart

You Will Need:

- pen, paper, and a ruler
- some masking tape

The Geology:

Geologists do **experiments** to identify the minerals in rocks they have found. Rocks can look very similar, but by carrying out a few simple tests they can work out what minerals they contain. Try it!

How To Make Your Chart

First, number your rock samples so you can identify them. Write each number on a piece of masking tape and stick a label onto each rock.

You will be conducting 13 experiments on your mystery rocks. Divide your paper into 14 columns. In the left hand column write your rock number. Write the experiment names along the top of your chart, starting in the second column. Now you are ready to record your results.

	Color	Hardness	Streak	Magnetism	Luster	Tranparency	Density	Texture	Scratch	Acidity	Cleavage	Absorbtion	Smell
Rock 1													
Rock 2													
Rock 3													

So Many Minerals!

There are thousands of different minerals found on Earth's surface and deep underground. Not everything that looks like a mineral is a mineral, and not every mineral looks like a rock. How do geologists decide what is a mineral and what isn't?

To be classed as a mineral, a substance must meet five requirements. It must be:

1. naturally occurring
2. inorganic
3. solid

And it must have:

4. a definite chemical composition
5. an ordered internal structure

"Naturally occurring" means it wasn't made by people, e.g. bronze is not a mineral. It is made when people mix tin and copper together.

"Inorganic" means not made by a living thing, e.g pearls are made by oysters so they cannot be minerals.

"Solid" means not a liquid or a gas at standard temperature and pressure. Water is not a mineral, but ice is.

"Definite chemical composition" means the mineral is always made in the same way, e.g. halite always has an equal number of atoms of the elements sodium and chlorine.

"Ordered internal structure" means its atoms are in a structured pattern, often seen in the shape of a mineral's crystals. Halite's sodium and chlorine atoms are arranged in a cube pattern. Its crystals are cube-shaped.

halite crystal

Think About This...

Do you know what common household substance is made from halite? You probably use it every day! Clue: halite is also known as rock salt.

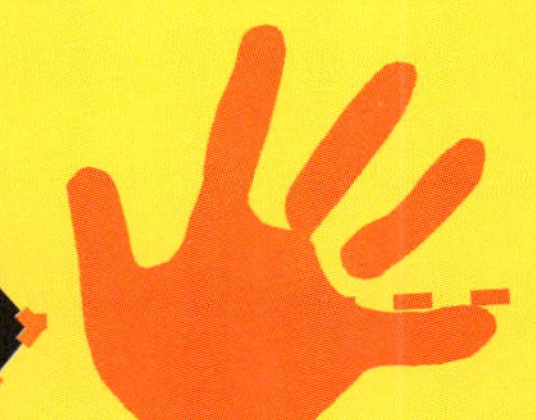

EXPERIMENT ONE
Identify Minerals By Their Hardness

You Will Need:

- a copper coin (some copper coins are not pure copper. A pre-1982 US penny or a pre-1992 UK penny are best)
- a steel nail
- some quartz if you have any

How To Test Your Rocks:

Try to scratch a specimen with your fingernail. Is the rock soft enough for your fingernail to leave a mark? If it does, look at the Mohs scale on the right. You'll see your rock might be talc or gypsum. If there was no mark, try scratching your specimen with a copper penny, and then a steel nail.

Scratching rock can create a powder that looks like a scratch. Rub any powder away. Can you still see a scratch?

If you are certain what a rock in your collection is, try scratching your specimen with that rock. If it leaves a mark, your specimen is softer on the scale, if it doesn't, it's harder.

The Geology:

Geologist Friedrich Mohs made a test to help identify minerals based on how hard or soft they are. Hard minerals will leave a scratch mark on softer ones. The Mohs' scale is a list of ten minerals, from softest to hardest.

1. Talc
2. Gypsum
3. Calcite
4. Fluorite
5. Apatite
6. Orthoclase Feldspar
7. Quartz
8. Topaz
9. Corundum
10. Diamond

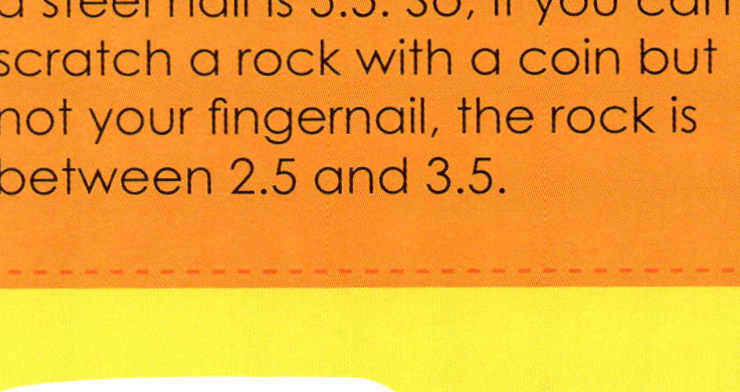

A fingernail is 2.5 on the Mohs scale. A copper coin is 3.5, and a steel nail is 5.5. So, if you can scratch a rock with a coin but not your fingernail, the rock is between 2.5 and 3.5.

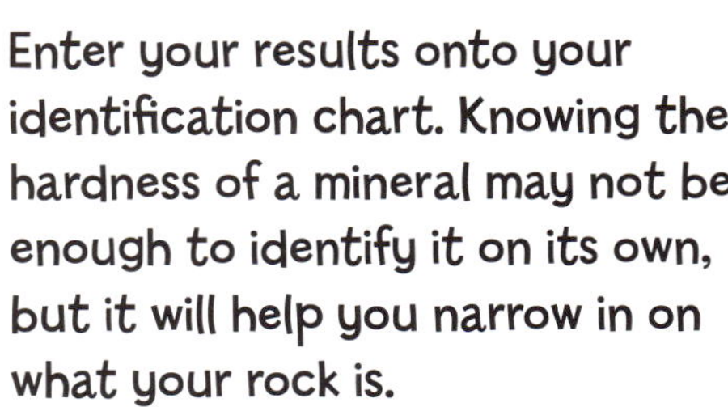

Enter your results onto your identification chart. Knowing the hardness of a mineral may not be enough to identify it on its own, but it will help you narrow in on what your rock is.

Metal Rocks

Around 99 percent of the minerals that make up Earth's crust are made from just eight elements. The elements are oxygen, silicon, aluminum, iron, calcium, sodium, potassium, and magnesium. Six of these elements are metals. The only non-metal is oxygen. Silicon is a metalloid, meaning it has properties that both metals and non-metals have. Other metals such as copper, silver, and gold can be found in rocks, too.

EXPERIMENT TWO
Is Your Rock Magnetic?

You Will Need:

- a selection of rocks
- a magnet
- a compass

How To Test For Magnetism:

Will the magnet stick to your rock? If not, hold it lightly between your thumb and index finger. Hold it near the rock. Can you feel a slight pull? Pass the rock slowly around a compass placed flat on a table. Does the compass needle move?

Think About This...

When a breakfast cereal says it contains minerals such as iron, does that mean we eat metal? Mix a cereal high in iron with water. Spoon the mush into a ziplock bag. If you move a neodymium magnet over the bag, eventually you might see a cluster of iron flecks following the magnet!

The Geology:

Iron is magnetic, and is a common element in most surface rocks. Iron will stick to a magnet and move a compass needle. Minerals containing a lot of iron can be magnetic. Magnetite and maghemite are strongly magnetic. Other minerals such as chromite, siderite, and ilmenite are slightly magnetic.

There are over 70 different metal chemical elements. Rocks that are rich in metals are called **ores**. Ores must be processed to get the metal out. The ore is crushed into small pieces and then cleaned. Then the ore is heated until the elements separate and liquid metal flows out. This process is called **smelting**. Sometimes people use electricity and chemicals to separate metal from ore. We also might mix metals together with other metals or nonmetals to produce new metal called **alloys**. Steel is an alloy of iron and carbon. Bronze is an alloy of copper and tin.

One way to identify if you have metal elements in your rock sample is to perform a streak test. Rubbing the rock along an unglazed tile or paving slab will leave a streak mark. The color of this mark can help identify minerals in the rock. You would think a rock would leave a streak that is the same color as the rock itself. However the surface of a rock can react with air, giving it a different color from the minerals within.

EXPERIMENT THREE
Sort Rocks Using a Streak Test

You Will Need:

- a selection of rocks
- a paving slab or an unglazed tile

The Geology:

Rocks don't always make the mark you expect. Pyrite and gold look really alike, but pyrite (known as fool's gold) makes a dark streak, whereas gold will make a gold-colored mark. Doing a streak test is a good way to easily tell them apart.

How To Do a Streak Test:

A streak test shows what color a rock would be if it was ground into a powder. You can help identify minerals by what color mark they make. Some minerals make quite distinctive marks. To do a streak test, take a clean rock and drag it very firmly across an unglazed tile or slab.

Mark Colour	Possible Mineral
metallic red	copper
black	magnetite
silver white	silver
white to grey	platinum
green	malachite
brown	hematite (iron oxide)

Rocks Can Be See-Through, Shiny, And They Can Even Glow!

The way a mineral reflects light is known as **luster**. Some rocks are shiny like metal, others are dull. Some rocks are completely see-through, too. The amount of light that can shine through a rock is known as a rock's **transparency**. The luster and transparency of a rock can help give you an idea what minerals it is made from.

HANDS-ON Can You Make a Rock Glow?

You Will Need:

- two rocks containing quartz
- eye protection
- a pair of pliers
- a dark room

A Native American tribe from Colorado filled buffalo hide rattles with quartz crystals. When the rattles were shaken at night the quartz crystals produced flashes of light!

IMPORTANT - wear eye protection as rock chips could fly into your face. Make sure the quartz is dry. Don't use your favorite crystals for this experiment as you will damage them. Most gravel has enough quartz in it for this experiment. In a dark room, firmly rub the two pieces of quartz together. You may see flashes of light. Now try striking one piece of quartz with the other. You should see small sparks. Try crushing a piece of quartz using pliers. You need a lot of pressure, but you may see the quartz glow.

What's happening? Squeezing the quartz crystals generates a tiny electric circuit. Light that is produced like this, by pressure or friction, is called **triboluminescence**.

EXPERIMENT FOUR
Luster and Transparency Tests

You Will Need:

- a desk lamp or strong daylight
- a magnifying glass
- a selection of minerals

How To Test for Luster:

Look at the surface of your mineral using a magnifying glass. Which of the words below best describes your mineral? Write the chosen word in the luster column in your table.

metallic - shines like metal and strongly reflects light.

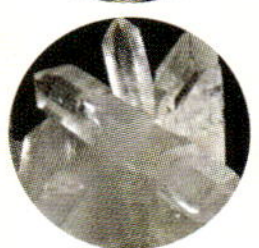

glassy - bright with a glassy shine.

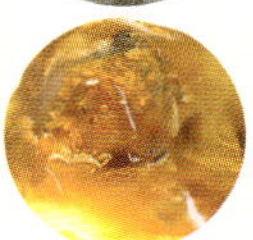

resinous - like tree sap or honey.

greasy - a dull sheen, as if it was coated with oil.

pearly - a whitish shimmer a little like a pearl.

silky- a sheen like silk material.

brilliant - a brilliant shine like a diamond.

dull - no shine

Testing For Transparency:

Hold your mineral up to the light. A mineral's transparency is how much light can pass through it. Choose a thin section, perhaps an edge or a corner, and look through the mineral toward your light source. Make a note in your table describing each mineral's transparency.

opaque

no light is passing through the mineral.

translucent

light is passing through the mineral but images are not clear.

transparent

light is passing through the mineral and images are clear.

The Geology:

Many minerals are transparent or translucent. Mica is so transparent it was used in windows! Gypsum is translucent and can have a pearly, glassy, greasy, or silky luster. Gold is opaque. Minerals with a metallic luster are always opaque.

Beautiful Gemstones

turquoise

emerald

Gemstones are minerals or rocks that have been cut, shaped, and polished. They are collected and used in jewelry. Emeralds, rubies, and sapphires are types of gemstone. Any attractive crystal can be cut into a gem. Most gemstones are made from naturally occurring crystals, but some organic materials such as amber and pearls are classed as gems, too. Gems are valued for their size, beauty, and how rare they are.

Some minerals produce more than one type of gem. Pure corundum is colorless. If corundum contains chromium it becomes a red ruby. If it contains titanium it becomes a blue sapphire. The best sapphires are colored by both titanium and iron.

a blue sapphire and red ruby

Quartz can produce gems of many colors – purple quartz is amethyst, yellow is citrine, brown is smoky quartz, and pink is rose quartz. Stripy agate and tiger eye are also quartz.

tiger eye

amethyst quartz

Metal elements give most gems their color. Chromium gives a ruby its deep red and gives emeralds their brilliant green. Iron gives the red, blue, and yellow colors to garnet, sapphire, and peridot. Copper gives the blue and green color to turquoise and malachite.

malachite

A diamond is a unique gem as it is made of just one chemical - carbon. Diamond is the hardest natural substance on Earth. The only thing that will cut a diamond is another diamond! Diamonds vary in color. Rare red and colorless are the most valuable.

Diamonds form between 75-120 miles (120-200 kms) below the Earth's crust. Over millions of years, extreme heat and pressure cause the carbon atoms to crystallize, forming diamonds. Volcanic eruptions then bring the diamonds to the surface.

Think About This...

Graphite, used in pencil lead, is also made of carbon atoms. Why is diamond the hardest mineral while graphite is one of the softest? Could it be how the carbon atoms are arranged?

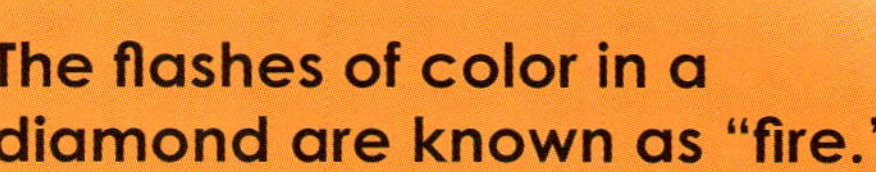

The flashes of color in a diamond are known as "fire."

HANDS-ON How To Polish Your Rocks

You Will Need:

- soft to medium-hard rocks
- fine sandpaper
- a tin or plastic container with a tight-fitting lid
- water
- coarse sand or grit
- cooking oil or car wax
- a scrap of fabric
- some patience!

Half-fill your container with coarse sand or grit. Add water until the container is two-thirds full. Place some rocks in the container that are similar in hardness. Tightly fit the lid. Now shake and roll the container for as long and often as you can, over several days. It can take weeks to make hard rocks smooth!

To make your rocks really smooth, sand them using a fine grain sandpaper. Wet the paper and gently sand each rock. Wipe away any dust.

Finally, dab some car wax or cooking oil onto a scrap of fabric. Gently polish the wax or oil into the stones. They should now look amazingly shiny.

Three Main Types of Rock

Geologists sort rocks into three main groups; **igneous**, **metamorphic**, and **sedimentary**.

- Igneous rocks form when molten rock deep within the Earth rises and cools.
- Metamorphic rocks have been changed by great heat and pressure under the surface of the Earth.
- Sedimentary rocks are made when sand, shells, and pebbles are carried by water, ice, or the wind. Known as sediment, this mixture settles by lakes, oceans, and deserts. Over millions of years it forms a layer of rock.

Think About This...

"Metamorphosis" means "change" in Greek. In Latin. "ignius" means "fire" and "sedere" means "to settle." If you can remember this, it may help you remember how each type of rock is formed.

Sedimentary Rock

When wind and water **erode** rock, the crumbling pieces of rock end up in streams and rivers that flow down the mountains. The pieces of rock and other matter are compressed and form sediment.

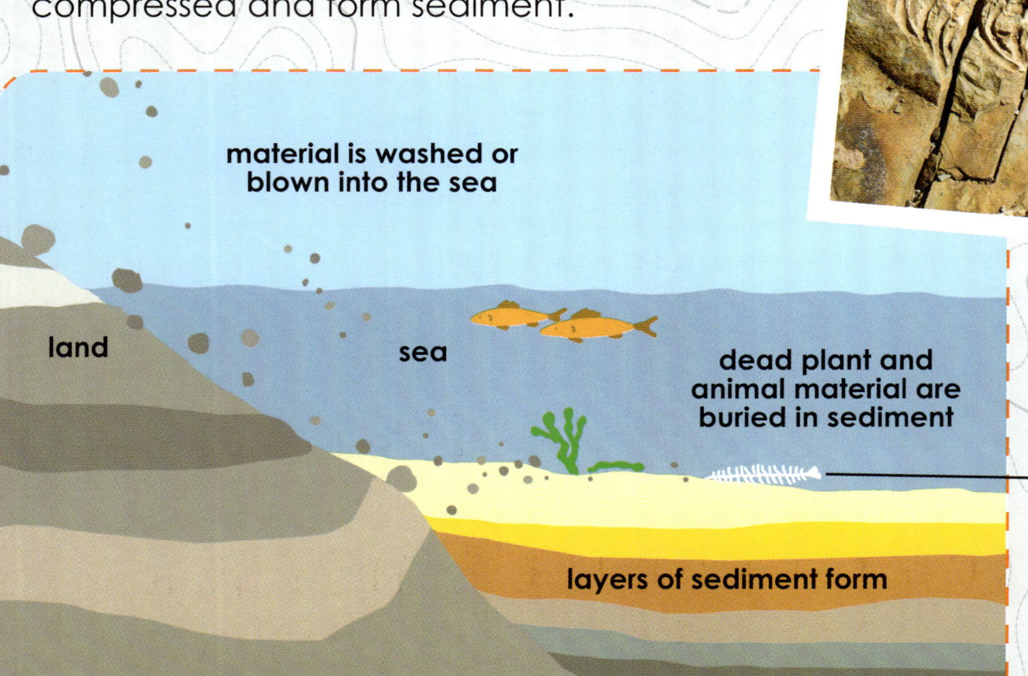

Dead animals and plants in the sediment can become preserved as fossils in the layers of sedimentary rock as it is compressed.

To tell if a rock sample is sedimentary, first see if you can find any fossils in it. Although other rock types can contain fossils, it is really very rare. Sedimentary rock is usually fairly soft and crumbly. You can sometimes see pebbles or stones cemented together in the rock. As sedimentary rock is formed in layers, you might see layers of different colors in the rock sample or at the place you found it.

fossils

limestone

conglomerate

sandstone

EXPERIMENT FIVE
Identify Rocks With an Acid Test

You Will Need:

- lemon juice or vinegar
- a glass
- some rock specimens
- magnifying glass
- eye protection

How To Do an Acid Test:

Wear eye protection, you don't want acid fizzing into your eyes. Pour half a cup of lemon juice or vinegar into a glass. Add your rock specimen.

Observe what happens using a magnifying glass. The rock may start to react with the liquid. It may fizz and create small bubbles.

The Geology:

Lemon juice and vinegar are acids. Acid dissolves carbonate found in some rocks. The reaction releases carbon dioxide gas in the form of small bubbles. If your rock fizzes, it contains carbonate.

Your rock could be limestone, chalk, or dolomite, which are sedimentary rocks. It could be marble, a metamorphic rock made when limestone is exposed to heat and pressure. It could be calcite or aragonite, which are found in all three types of rock.

Beware–some rocks, such as sandstone, have holes that trap pockets of air. The escaping air can appear to fizz, but sandstone does not contain carbonate. Double check the reaction by scratching some rock onto a plate and spooning the acid onto the powder.

Igneous Rock

Our planet, Earth, is made mostly of a large mass of igneous rock with a very thin layer of sedimentary rock on top. While sedimentary rocks are produced by processes at Earth's surface, both igneous and metamorphic rocks are formed deep under the ground.

Think About This...

Devils Tower, Wyoming is an example of igneous rock. Created underground by a volcano around 50 million years ago, the hot magma cooled creating this amazing rock with hexagonal-shaped columns. Originally formed underground, why do you think Devils Tower is now above ground?

How can you tell if you have igneous rocks in your rock collection? Examine your specimens. What do you see?

Large crystals? Igneous rocks can be formed when molten magma cools deep inside the Earth. The rocks gradually work their way to the surface. Known as **intrusive**, or **plutonic**, igneous rock, the slow cooling means large crystals get trapped in the rock. An example of this type of rock is granite.

granite

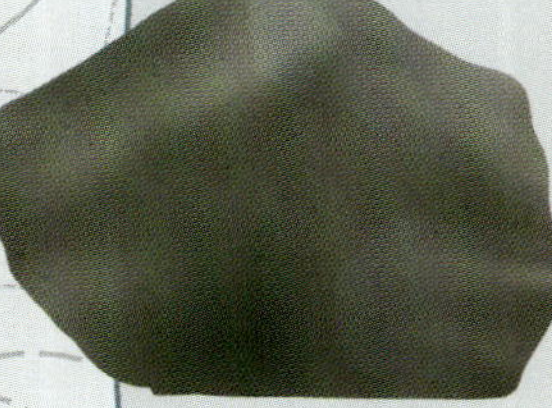

basalt

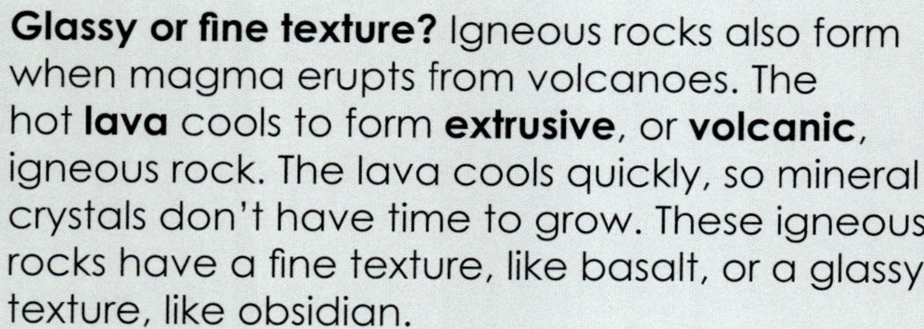

Glassy or fine texture? Igneous rocks also form when magma erupts from volcanoes. The hot **lava** cools to form **extrusive**, or **volcanic**, igneous rock. The lava cools quickly, so mineral crystals don't have time to grow. These igneous rocks have a fine texture, like basalt, or a glassy texture, like obsidian.

obsidian

Holes? Hot gas bubbles can get trapped in lava, leaving tiny holes in the rock. Pumice and scoria are good examples of this type of igneous rock.

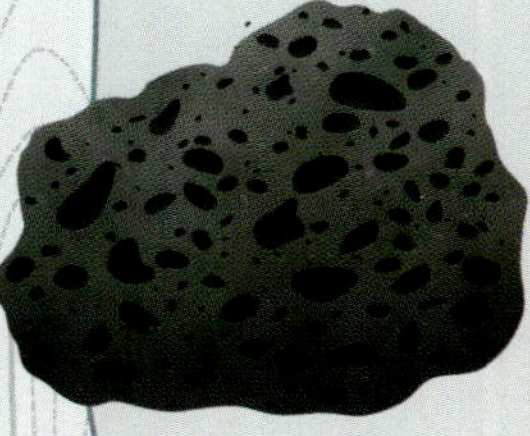

scoria

EXPERIMENT SIX
Measuring Specific Gravity

Specific gravity is a measurement of the **density** of something. To work out what a specimen's specific gravity is, we need to measure the density of the sample, and then compare that to the density of an equal volume of water. How? Try making your own Jolly Balance.

You Will Need:

- a stick
- books
- string
- a spring from a ballpoint pen
- paper fastener
- a ruler
- a large jar half-full of water
- rocks smaller than half the jar

How To Test Your Rocks:

Rest a stick across two equal height piles of books. Hook or tie one end of the spring to the stick. Tie one end of a piece of string to the rock sample. Tie the other end to the bottom of the spring. Clip an opened paper fastener on the string. Secure a ruler next to your dangling rock. Record where the paper clip pointer points to on your ruler. Lift the rock and place the jar of water under it. Lower the rock into the jar. Record the paper clip pointer reading again.

The Geology:

Most minerals in the Earth's crust have very similar densities, of around 2.6 to 3.0 grams per cubic cm. Metallic samples are usually the densest. Some elements such as iridium and platinum can have densities as high as 20! Rocks can have a range of densities, as different specimens may contain different amounts of each mineral. Granite can be between 20 and 60 percent quartz.

Rock	Specific Gravity
Sandstone	2.2–2.8
Granite	2.6-2.7
Basalt	2.8-3.0
Iron Ore	4.5-5.3
Lead Ore	7.5

To calculate the specific gravity of your rock, divide the first reading by the first reading minus the second reading:

$$\frac{\text{Weight of Mineral in Air [20]}}{\text{Weight of Mineral in Air [20] - Weight of Mineral in Water [15]}} \quad (20-15 = 5)$$

20 divided by 5 is 5, so our sample might be Iron Ore.

This metamorphic rock face in Japan was created when layers of sandstone and shale were heated and compressed to create this banded hornfel rock.

Metamorphic Rock

Metamorphic rock is formed from other rock that is changed by heat and pressure deep under the surface of Earth. Metamorphic rock originally could have been sedimentary or igneous rock, or older metamorphic rock. The heat and pressure rearranges the elements to form new minerals. The conditions underground have to be just right. Too much heat or pressure and the rock will melt, become magma, and form igneous rock instead.

Metamorphic rocks have what is known as parent rocks - that is, a rock that they were formed from. For instance marble might be formed from limestone or dolomite. Slate is formed from shale or occasionally from basalt.

Think About This...

Metamorphic rocks can be made from sedimentary rocks that contain fossils. Metamorphic rocks rarely contain fossils though. Why do you think that might be?

Gneiss

Parent rocks:

shale

granite

Gneiss has banded layers of different minerals. Parent rocks can be shale, sandstone, feldspar, quartz, mica or granite! It is often used for building and paving.

Marble

Parent rocks:

limestone

dolomite

Marble is a hard rock made of crystals. Impurities can color marble gray, black, red, green, pink, banded and mottled! It is used for sculpture and building.

Slate

Parent rocks:

shale

basalt

Slate is formed at a lower pressure and temperature than many metamorphic rocks. It naturally splits into fine sheets making it perfect for roof tiles.

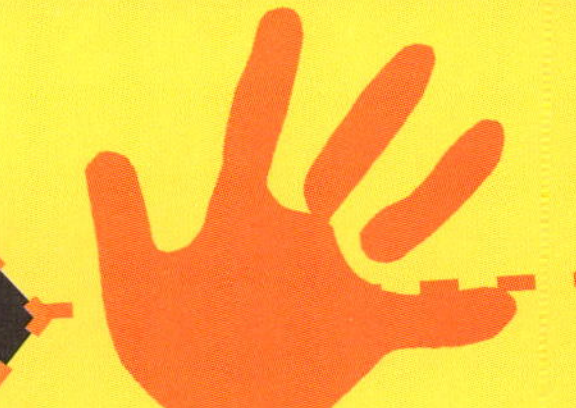

EXPERIMENT SEVEN
Testing Cleavage and Fracture

How a rock or mineral breaks into pieces can give you a clue to what it is. If it breaks along flat surfaces, that is called **cleavage**. If it breaks and creates uneven surfaces that is known as **fracture**.

You Will Need:

- minerals you are happy to break
- two towels
- a hard outdoor floor area
- a hammer
- eye protection
- gloves

adult help needed

How To Test Your Minerals:

To test your mineral samples, lay a towel on the ground on a hard surface. Place the sample on the towel. Cover the sample with the other towel. IMPORTANT - put on eye protection as the towel may not catch all the flying pieces. Wear gloves, as fragments may be sharp.

Hit your covered sample with the hammer. Lift up the top towel and examine your pieces. Can you see a flat-edged shape? Then you are looking at cleavage. Or are there uneven fragments? Record the look and texture of the pieces on your mineral chart.

The Geology:

The mineral galena will break into perfect cubes. This is known as cleavage along three planes. Why three? Because parallel surfaces count as the same plane! Mica's cleavage is in one plane, as mica will break into thin sheets. The kind of cleavage a mineral has is because of its structure not its original shape. A six-sided crystal will actually fracture, not create six flat surfaces!

Minerals that do not break into geometric shapes will fracture instead. Minerals can fracture into all kinds of irregular shapes. Some create bowl-shaped curves with sharp edges. Look at the fracture surfaces. Some are smooth, and some are rough, some can look like needles or splinters.

Think About This...

Early man made tools and weapons from flint fragments. How do you think flint would fracture?

The Great Rock ReCycle

We know that metamorphic rocks change, but do you think an igneous rock will always be an igneous rock? Over time, <u>all</u> rocks actually change from one type to another. How? Forces inside the Earth gradually move the underground igneous and metamorphic rocks to the surface. On the surface they get weathered and eroded. Other forces then compact them and sink them back down, where they are heated and pressed into sedimentary rock, or melted to form magma. In this way, all the minerals that make up Earth's rocks are constantly being recycled.

Think About This...

Earth is 4.6 billion years old. Most of its early crust has been recycled several times since the planet formed. However, in 2008, scientists found some rock in Northern Quebec that has remained unchanged for 4.28 billion years!

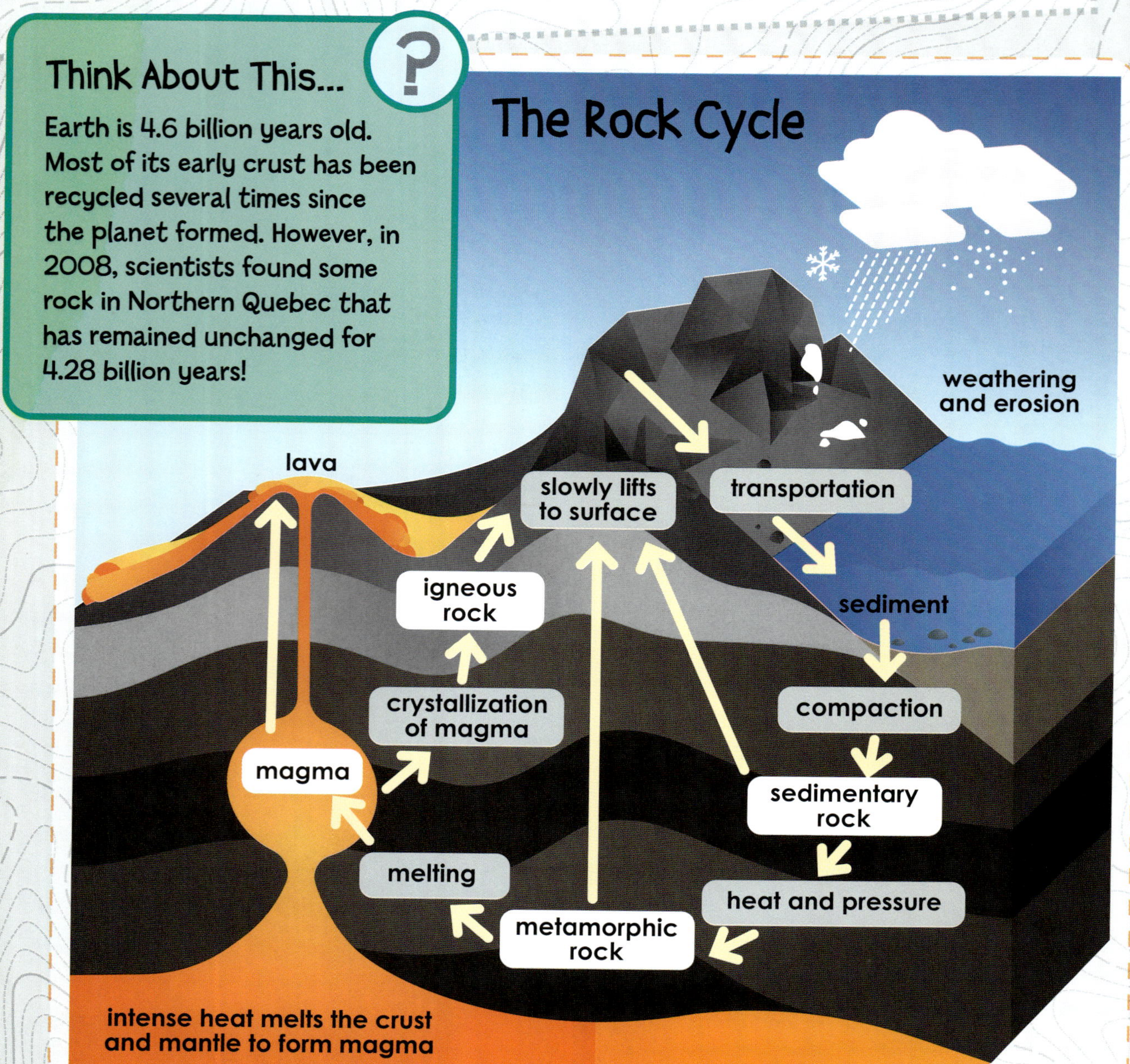

EXPERIMENT EIGHT
Bake a Chocolate Rock Cycle

You Will Need:

- white and milk chocolate
- a cheese grater
- bowl
- spoon
- aluminum foil
- baking tray
- an oven heated to 200F (90C)
- bowl of hot water

adult help needed

The Geology:

The grater turned the chocolate "rock" into smaller pieces, just as rock is eroded and weathered in nature. Our sedimentary rock was made by pressure on the eroded chocolate. The force of being pressed into the mold and the heat of the oven created our metamorphic chocolate rock. Igneous rock was made when our melted chocolate "magma" cooled.

How To Make Them:

To mimic rock erosion, grate some white and dark chocolate into the same bowl. Ask an adult to help you as graters are sharp. Divide the chocolate shavings into three equal portions.

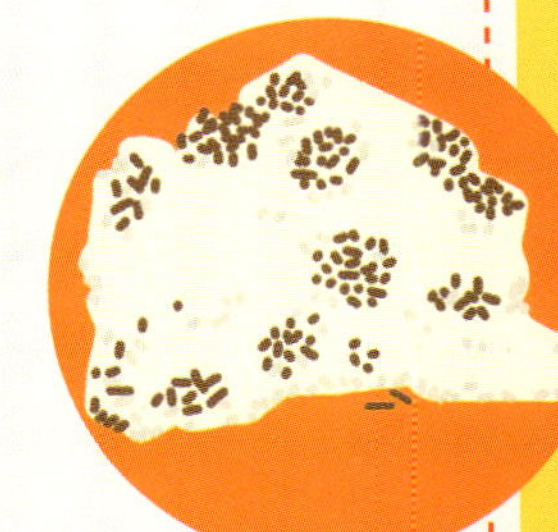

To make your sedimentary rock, press one of the portions of grated chocolate together using the back of a spoon.

To make metamorphic rock, create a rock-shaped mold out of foil. Press the second portion of grated chocolate into the mold. Put the mold on a baking tray. Put in the oven for a couple of minutes until the chocolate has melted. Leave to cool.

Now make your igneous rock. Ask an adult to help fill a cup with boiling water. Wrap the last portion of grated chocolate in some foil and carefully lower it into the water. After a few minutes lift the foil out. Put it in the refrigerator to harden. Then unwrap your "rock."

Amazing Crystals

Crystals form when a liquid, such as magma, cools and hardens. The **molecules** in the liquid pull together in a repeating pattern, creating each crystal's shape. Crystals form beautiful, unique shapes. Snowflakes, diamonds, and table salt are examples of crystals. Crystals can also form when water evaporates from a chemical mixture. Salt crystals form when salt water evaporates.

These enormous gypsum crystals were found recently at a mine in Naica, Mexico.

Rocks' building blocks

A mineral's crystal structure is as important as the elements it contains. Graphite is the soft, dark material used in pencil lead. Diamond is a hard, often colorless, gemstone. These two minerals are very different, and yet they are both made from pure carbon.

They are different because they have completely different crystal structures. Graphite forms loosely bonded sheets which rub off as you draw with a pencil. Diamond forms a tightly stacked cubic crystal structure.

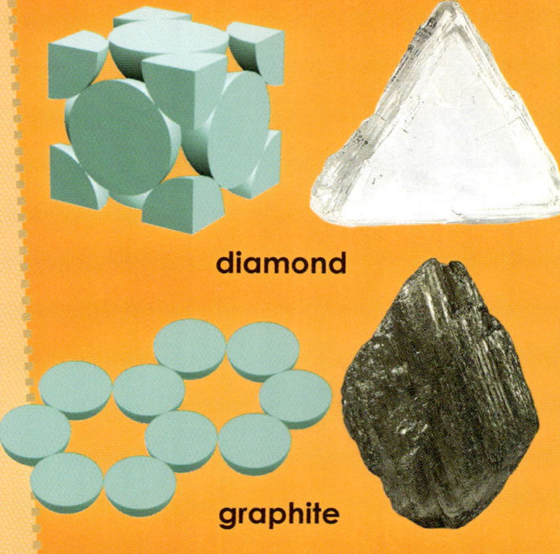

HANDS-ON Marshmallow Crystals

You Will Need:
- toothpicks
- marshmallows

halite

Halite, known as rock salt, forms cube-shaped crystals. Try creating its crystal structure using marshmallows and toothpicks! Halite, like table salt, is made from sodium and chlorine. You could use different color marshmallows for each element.

Geodes are round, ordinary-looking rocks with a hole inside lined with minerals. The outer rock is hard, allowing the geode to survive if the surrounding rock weathers away. Geodes can be lined with quartz or calcite crystals, colorful bands of agate, purple amethyst, and other beautiful minerals. You can buy geodes from rock stores to crack open yourself with a hammer!

EXPERIMENT NINE
Grow Your Own Crystal Geode

You Will Need:

adult help needed

- two tumblers
- boiling water
- food coloring
- alum powder (in the grocery store spice section)
- a measuring cup and spoon
- an egg

The Geology:

Rock geodes take thousands of years to form. This experiment speeds it up a little! As the warm alum solution cools, the particles of alum fall to the bottom and start to turn into crystals. Coating the shell with alum powder gives the particles a friendly surface to attach to. Your eggshell geode is created in the same way sedimentary rock is created. Particles in a liquid will settle against a barrier, whether that is the bottom of the ocean, or the side of an eggshell!

How To Make Your Geode:

Gently crack an egg into a tumbler so the shell splits in half. Carefully peel off the membrane from inside one half. Rinse it and let it dry.

Ask an adult to pour one cup of boiling water into the other tumbler. Add four tablespoons of alum to the water and stir until the alum dissolves. Add a few drops of food coloring.

Sprinkle some alum powder inside the half eggshell. Submerge the shell, open side up, so it rests at the bottom of the glass of alum solution.

After several hours, sparkling crystals should have formed inside your eggshell geode!

Some Very Unusual Rocks

There are some rocks which have unusual properties. Try some of the tests on this page and see if any of your collection absorb water, make you see double, or maybe just smell weird!

Viking sunstone

EXPERIMENT TEN
Do Rocks Absorb Water?

You Will Need:

- some rocks including pumice, chalk, or sandstone
- a measuring jug or beaker
- water
- a set of scales
- a pen and paper
- some foil

The Geology:

Rocks such as granite have grains that fit tightly together. They do not absorb water.

Rocks with rounded, loose grains, such as sandstone; or holes, such as pumice, will absorb water.

In some areas, water stored in layers of rock, known as aquifers, is pumped to the surface and used as drinking water.

How To Check Absorbancy:

Weigh your rock sample. Write down the result. Fill a measuring jug or beaker with enough water to cover the rock. Record the amount of water.

Carefully place your rock into the water. You don't want to splash any water out. Cover the jug with foil to prevent evaporation.

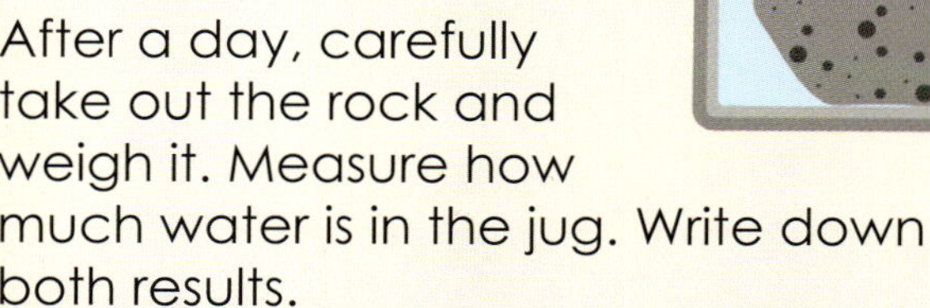

After a day, carefully take out the rock and weigh it. Measure how much water is in the jug. Write down both results.

If your rock weighs the same, and the water levels stayed the same, then your specimen probably isn't absorbent.

Think About This...

Did any of your rocks float? Why do you think that might happen?

HANDS-ON Identify By Smell!

You Will Need:
- any of the following: sulfur, pyrite, kaolinite, jet, or amber
- a needle

adult help needed

Some minerals and elements give off a distinctive odor. Sulfur and pyrite smell a little like when someone strikes a match. If you hit two pieces together, they smell like bad eggs! If you smell garlic instead, put the rock down and wash your hands. You have found an arsenopyrite specimen, which contains the poison, arsenic!

Clay minerals such as kaolinite smell like fresh clay when damp.

If you have a jet or amber specimen that you don't mind poking a hole in, ask an adult to heat a needle and stick it in the specimen. Jet smells like burning tar and amber smells like burning pine sap. Jet and amber aren't actually minerals. Jet is compressed wood and amber is tree resin.

A type of calcite known as Iceland spar makes you see double! When light passes through the crystals, it is split into two rays. The two beams are bent by different amounts, causing a double image.

It is believed Viking navigators used the stone to help tell where the Sun was on cloudy days. How? They marked a dot on the stone. If they looked through the stone they would see two dots. Looking through the stone, they moved it along the horizon. They saw two dots until the stone lined up directly under the Sun. Then the rings of light that surround the Sun, even under cloudy skies, would cause the second dot to disappear.

If you placed a specimen of Iceland spar on some type, you would see double!

Vikings called Iceland spar "sunstone."

Can You Identify Your Rocks?

Look at your experiment results and see if you can identify your rock samples using this chart. If you don't think your specimen is listed, ask an adult if they can help you try an internet search. Type in your results, such as "gray banded rock," "large grains", "white streak test," "waxy luster" and you may find your rock that way.

Name	Color	Hardness	Streak
agate	all colors, multicolored, or banded	6.5-7	white
apatite	yellow, green, blue, brown	5	white
basalt	gray to black or brown	6	white - gray
calcite	mainly colorless or white	3	white
conglomerate	tan to brown	2-3	white
corundum	many colors or colorless	9	white
dolomite	white, gray, pink or brownish white	3.5-4	white
feldspar	pink, white, gray, brown, blue	6-6.5	white
flint	gray, black, brown, red, white	6.5-7	white
fluorite	colorless or colored by impurities	4	white
galena	lead gray and silvery	2.5-2.7	lead gray
granite	red, pink, gray, or white	6-7	white
graphite	black to silver-gray	1-2	black
gypsum	colorless, white, gray, yellow, red, brown	2	white
halite	clear, white, red, or orange	2.5	white
hematite	black, silver gray or red to brown	5-6	red brown
limestone	white or almost white	3-4	white
magnetite	black or gray with a brown tint	5.5-6.5	black
malachite	bright, dark, or blackish green	3.5-4	light green
marble	black, blue, brown, grey, pink, white	3-4	white
mica	colorless, transparent, or many colors	2-4	white/none
obsidian	deep black or blackish green	5-6	white
olivine	olive, bright, or yellowish green	6.5-7	none
pumice	usually white, cream, blue, or grey	6	white/green
pyrite	brassy yellow	6-6.5	green/black
quartz	colorless, transparent, or many colors	7	white
sandstone	gray, yellow, red, or white	6-7	white
scoria	dark brown, purple, or black	5-6	white
shale	usually gray	3	white
slate	gray, black, with blue, brown, green	3-4	brown
talc	Light to dark green, white, grey, colorless	1	white

Igneous, sedimentary, metamorphic?

- If your rock has layers it is a metamorphic or sedimentary rock.
- Only sedimentary rocks, and very rarely metamorphic rocks, contain fossils.
- Only sedimentary rocks will have complete fossils.
- Sedimentary rocks' crystals are easily broken or scratched.
- Metamorphic rocks are usually brittle and lightweight, igneous rocks are dense and hard.

Luster	S. Gravity	Other properties
waxy	2.6	sharp fracture
glassy	3.2	six-sided crystals
dull	2.8-3	fine grain
glassy/pearly	2.7	reacts to acid test
dull	2.8	coarse grain with gravel lumps
glassy/brilliant	3.9-4.1	mostly see-through
glassy/pearly	2.8	might react to acid test
glassy	2.6-2.8	cleavage along two or three planes
waxy/dull	2.7	fractures with sharp edges
glassy	3.2	may be fluorescent
metallic	5.4	cleavage creates perfect cubes
mainly dull	2.7	dark mineral grains
metallic	1.8-2.3	has a greasy feel and smudges
glassy/silky	2.3-2.7	water soluble, splits into thin sheets
dull/glassy	2.1-2.6	salty taste, cubic cleavage
metallic/dull	5.2-5.3	may easily break off finto lakes
dull/pearly	2.3-2.7	fine grain, soluble in water and acid
metallic	5.2	strongly magnetic
brilliant/glassy/dull	3.6-4	forms green bands
dull/pearly	2.9	might react to acid test
pearly/glassy	2.8-3	splits into thin sheets
glassy	2.4	fractures with very sharp edges
glassy	3.2-4.4	found in many meteorites
dull	2.9	fine grains, holes, floats, absorbs water
metallic	4.9-5.2	can form different-shaped crystals
glassy/waxy/dull	2.6	some quartz crystals glow if pressed
dull	2.2-2.8	gritty, will absorb water
glassy/dull	1	features bubble-like holes
dull	2.6	fine grains, breaks into thin layers
dull	2.5	breaks into thin layers, rings if struck
waxy/pearly	2.6-2.8	very soft, scratched by a fingernail

Glossary

alloys a substance of two or more metals or a metal and nonmetal united usually by being melted together.

atoms the smallest particles of an element, having all the characteristics of that element.

cleavage the tendency for a rock or mineral to break along a flat surface.

core the central part of the Earth.

crust the outer part of the Earth.

crystals a solid form of a substance or mixture that has a regularly repeating internal arrangement of its atoms and often external plane faces.

density the mass per unit volume.

earthquakes a shaking or trembling of a portion of the Earth's surface.

elements fundamental substances that consist of atoms of only one kind and that cannot be separated into simpler substances.

erode to wear away by or as if by the action of water, wind, or glacial ice.

experiments procedures or operations carried out under controlled conditions in order to discover something.

extrusive formed by a volcano in a melted state or as volcanic ash.

fluorescence giving off radiation usually as visible light when exposed to radiation from another source.

fracture any separation in a rock, such as a joint or fault that divides the rock into two or more pieces.

geodes stones having a cavity lined with crystals or mineral matter.

geology a science that deals with the history of the Earth and its life especially as recorded in rocks.

igneous formed by hardening of melted Earth.

inorganic composed of matter that does not come from plants or animals either alive or dead.

intrusive having been forced while melted into cavities or between layers.

lava melted rock coming from a volcano.

luster a shine or sheen especially from reflected light.

mantle the portion of the Earth lying between the crust and the core.

metamorphic changed into a more compact form by the action of pressure, heat, and water.

minerals solid chemical compounds that occur naturally in the form of crystals.

molecules the simplest unit of a chemical substance, usually a group of two or more atoms.

opaque not letting light through.

ores minerals mined to obtain a substance they contain.

phosphorescence a light given off at low temperatures caused by the absorption of radiation and continuing for a time after these radiations have stopped.

plutonic relating to igneous rock formed by solidification at considerable depth beneath the Earth's surface.

sedimentary formed by or from sediment.

smelting to melt usually in order to separate the metal.

specimens a portion of material for use in testing or examination.

translucent not transparent but clear enough to allow light to pass through.

transparency being transparent.

transparent may be seen through.

triboluminescence the emission of light from a substance caused by rubbing.

volcanic relating to, or produced by a volcano.

volcano a vent in the Earth's crust from which melted or hot rock and steam come out.

Further Information

Museums and Places to Visit

Visit a museum. Most big city museums will have exhibits and information about local rocks and minerals.

Visit local rock shops. Enthusiasts love sharing their information.

L**ook for beginners geology classes.** If a college in your area teaches geology it may put on classes for young people.

Useful Websites

Try doing this National Geographic quiz on rocks and minerals
https://kids.nationalgeographic.com/games/quizzes/quiz-whiz-rocks-minerals/

The Geological Society have plenty of information about rocks and the rock cycle
https://www.geolsoc.org.uk/ks3/gsl/education/resources/rockcycle/page3445.html

https://www.geolsoc.org.uk/ks3/gsl/education/resources/rockcycle.html

Kids Love Rocks has plenty of information on crystals, rock types, and how to make a rock collection
https://kidsloverocks.com/types-of-rock

Books to Read

Dennie, Devin. *My Book of Rocks and Minerals: Things to Find, Collect, and Treasure*. London, UK: DK Children, 2017.

Honovich, Nancy. *Ultimate Explorer Field Guide: Rocks and Minerals*. Washington, DC, USA: National Geographic Kids, 2016.

Index